Mark H. Law is a balance consultant, who lives in Sydney, Australia.

To all the people that have made the world a better place.

Mark H. Law

21ST CENTURY BALANCE

Unconventional Wisdom to Enlighten
Yourself and Inspire Others

AUSTIN MACAULEY PUBLISHERS™
LONDON * CAMBRIDGE * NEW YORK * SHARJAH

Copyright © Mark H. Law 2022

The right of Mark H. Law to be identified as author of this work has been asserted by the author in accordance with sections 77 and 78 of the Copyright, Designs and Patents Act 1988.

All rights reserved. No part of this publication may be reproduced, stored in a retrieval system or transmitted in any form or by any means, electronic, mechanical, photocopying, recording or otherwise, without the prior permission of the publishers.

Any person who commits any unauthorised act in relation to this publication may be liable to criminal prosecution and civil claims for damages.

The story, experiences, and words are the author's alone.

A CIP catalogue record for this title is available from the British Library.

ISBN 9781398441675 (Paperback)
ISBN 9781398441682 (ePub e-book)

www.austinmacauley.com

First Published 2022
Austin Macauley Publishers Ltd®
1 Canada Square
Canary Wharf
London
E14 5AA

Table of Contents

Introduction: The Purpose of Balance — 11

Chapter 1: What Makes You Most Happy? — 17

   Predictors of Happiness — 18

   Life Satisfaction as a Form of Happiness — 19

   Circumstances Influencing Life Satisfaction — 21

   The Setting of Expectations — 23

   The Phenomenology of Human Compassion — 25

   Happiness as a State of Mind — 26

   The Relative State of Happiness — 27

   The Equilibrium State of Mind — 29

   Key Points — 31

Chapter 2: Social Media Renaissance — 33

   History of Social Media — 33

   Effect of Social Media Platforms — 34

   Achieving the Equilibrium of Validation — 37

   Descartes's Method of Doubt — 39

   Extroversion, Introversion and Ambiversion — 40

   Key Points — 44

Chapter 3: The Optimal Goal Strategy — 46

   Innate Potential — 48

The Optimal Goal	*50*
The Equilibrium of Pursuit	*52*
Strategies of Self-Awareness	*55*
1. Where do You Spend Your Time?	*55*
2. What Are Your Natural Inclinations?	*56*
3. What Goals Are Worth Your Struggle?	*56*
4. Further Your Awareness from External Sources	*57*
5. Who Do You Aspire to Become?	*57*
Benefits of Self-Awareness	*58*
Going Backwards Before Going Forward	*58*
Key Points	*60*
Chapter 4: The Balance of Change	**61**
The First Industrial Revolution	*61*
Informed Change Analysis	*64*
Steps Of the Informed Change Analysis	*65*
Habits Of Change	*67*
The Progressive Mindset	*69*
The Progressive Mindset of Ludwig Van Beethoven	*73*
The Twenty-First Century Environment	*75*
Key Points	*81*
Chapter 5: Inspire Yourself or Who Will?	**83**
The Story of The Wright Brothers	*83*
The Self-Belief of The Wright Brothers	*88*
The Value of Self-Belief	*90*
Strategies to Develop Self-Belief	*91*
1. Reinforcing Your Foundations	*91*
2. The Paradigm Shift of Knowledge	*92*

3. Assess and Replace Negative Thoughts	92
4. Reinforce with Your Body Language	93
Cultivating Character	93
Key Points	96

Chapter 6: The Enhanced Perspective — 97

The Art of Purpose	97
Interrelationships	101
Valuable Character Traits	101
Types of Listening	102
Disagreements and Mutual Appreciation	103
Debate and Discussion	104
Leonardo's Enhanced Perspective	106
Types of Heuristics	108
1. Availability Heuristic	109
2. Representativeness Heuristic	109
3. Affect Heuristic	110
Key Points	112

Chapter 7: Emphasise Your Belief System — 114

The Philosophical Movement of Stoicism	114
Existing Belief Systems	116
Beliefs of Stoicism	118
Direct Your Focus on What You can Control	118
The Obstacles You Face are an Opportunity that Leads to Advancement	118
Act in Accordance with Ethical Principles	119
Being Appreciative in Your Actions	120
Practice the Values and Embody Them	120

The Motivations for Human Needs	*122*
Key Points	*125*
Chapter 8: How to Remain Content	**127**
Nelson Mandela's Path to Presidency	*129*
Utilitarian Third-Person Analysis	*135*
Becoming Your Own Best Friend	*137*
Gratitude	*139*
Steps to Practice Gratitude	*139*
1. Develop Mindfulness	*139*
2. Exercise Meditation	*139*
3. Express Your Gratefulness	*140*
4. Recall Grateful Experiences	*140*
Key Points	*141*
Chapter 9: Attaining the Twenty-First Century Balance	**143**
The Evaluation of Henry Ford	*146*
Harmony	*148*
Conclusion	**150**
Progress Forward from Here	*150*
References	**152**

Introduction
The Purpose of Balance

The twenty-first century has seen a shift in the modern culture due to technological and social developments. We are now increasingly immersed in our smartphones—through the internet, we are able to browse according to our interests, read the news and engage with people over social media.

There has never been a period in history where people are exposed to so much information all at once. While the overall human condition has improved, as evident in the decline of global poverty since the late twentieth century, an increasing number of people are experiencing depression.

The improvement in the human condition does not pertain to the improvements made to achieve happiness.

The circumstances in the twenty-first century create a range of new problems that require the solution of balance:

1. The pursuit toward obtaining happiness is endorsed within our culture. To satisfy your desires, you strive toward obtaining the next best product or experience. However, when is it time to take a step back to relax and begin living with gratitude? This raises the question, what is more worthwhile than striving toward the pursuit of happiness?
2. Interacting on social media platforms increases the number of engagements you have with people online. However, after using these platforms over long periods of time, you have since not received any emotional improvements in the state of your well-being.
   You, now make an intentional effort to reduce your social media use but it is still not effective. The goal should be to use social media to interact with individuals without experiencing its negative effects.

3. When you begin to experience monotony in your daily routine and it all feels tiresome, this leads you to pursue your aspirations. Due to the ongoing distractions however, it becomes a challenge to maintain this new routine.

   You start to hesitate pursuing the aspiration, and you begin to ask yourself, "How can I accomplish the right commitment that removes the uncertainties in my life?"
4. You have seen your friends or acquaintances fulfil their goals and desires in a balanced state of mind. You congratulate their accomplishments with sincerity, but afterwards, you contemplate whether they achieved the success through luck or self-alignment.
5. Change is currently taking place in your life from your career, relationships or circumstances. You feel overwhelmed by this transition and you can't decide whether you want to return to the past experience or move forward with confidence.

   Through this experience, you learn how to manage change, but you don't know whether the outcome was worthwhile. What you do know is that you would just like to be at peace with yourself.
6. You are busy with your life and have many commitments including work, family and your personal interests. You intend to make some changes, but you are uncertain about whether you have enough time to fulfil your responsibilities.

   You've researched your intended pursuits, but you still do not have the assurance that fulfilling the changes will bring you contentment.
7. There are moments in your life where you acknowledged that it is optimal to remain content with what you experienced. You try to retain such gratitude, but over time, you repeat the pursuit of another desire.

Finding balance in your life provides the *pragmatic* solution in addressing your challenges. To obtain purpose and long-term fulfilment requires long-term thinking. The focus toward making the right decisions requires knowledge about yourself such that you are able to align yourself toward developing the right objectives.

Your circumstances are determined by how you choose to respond to situations that has resulted in the current outcome. But have you ever pursued a balanced state of living and being, a state that aligns your natural capabilities with the external opportunities? This is the secret—it is how people have been able to self-actualise.

Over the course of history, many individuals have pursued this balanced state of living. These notable individuals include: Napoleon Bonaparte, the Wright brothers, Leo Tolstoy, Leonardo da Vinci, Aristotle, Socrates, Nelson Mandela and Henry Ford.

Through an analysis of their journeys and experiences, you will learn the strategies and processes in order to achieve your own state of balance. This will allow you to become one step closer to attaining fulfilment in your life such that you can live in balance.

This book outlines historical analysis combined with scientific research in order to outline the strategies that are applicable for the modern context. It is through these different types of knowledge, applied within your appropriate timing that becomes a part of your own inner wisdom.

Balance is a wide-ranging topic that cannot be simply defined over a single thesis. Instead, the formulas used to achieve balance are presented. There are two types of balance: namely the external and internal balance. To obtain the external balance you must pursue the commitments that are in alignment with your character.

Conversely, while you are not engaging in your commitments or interacting in your relationships, you can pursue an internal balance, which allows you to live in the state of peace. Through combining both your internal and external states of balance, you will then live in harmony.

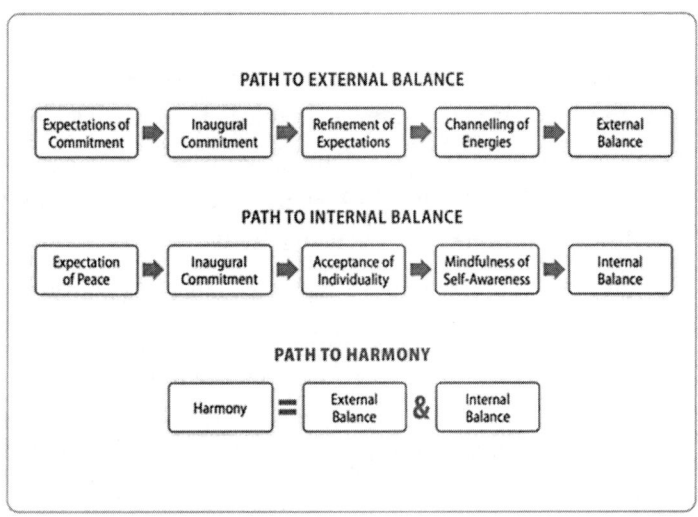

The paths to achieving the internal and external states of balance are outlined, and each of the journeys involve the undertaking of its own challenges. To obtain a comprehensive solution and to set expectations, requires you to strive for the right commitment.

For the external balance, every person is required to have their own self-awareness of recognising their strengths, weaknesses and natural inclinations.

As a result, the external balance involves pursuing the commitment that is in alignment with your personal values and long-term objectives, which allows you to obtain the results that you desire.

Conversely, internal balance requires you to live in the equilibrium state of mind. This involves establishing the strategies and processes to live at peace. In a world that is now filled with information and distractions, it is challenging to determine where it is optimal to focus your attention.

It is through your ability to regulate your thoughts, sentiments, and beliefs, combined with accepting who you are on a personal level that will allow you to remain content. This process will result in you being able to obtain your internal balance so you can live in the present moment.

To live harmoniously requires the knowledge obtained from the content presented in this book. Each chapter focuses on a specific topic.

Chapter 1: Evaluates the relative state of happiness to determine whether its pursuit is worthwhile. Through outlining psychological research to analyse life satisfaction between cultures and the effects of setting expectations, the practice of compassion is then presented.

This focuses towards the equilibrium state of mind and its long-term benefits of redefining one's purpose.

Chapter 2: Discusses the history and analysis of social media platforms. Research from the field of psychology is presented to examine the effects of social media use in people's validation dependency and well-being.

Strategies to use social media proficiently are outlined to allow you to connect with other users without experiencing the drawbacks.

Chapter 3: Outlines the strategies to increase your own self-awareness, so you can be informed of your innate characteristics and the worthwhile objectives to pursue.

Chapter 4: Presents an overview of the first industrial revolution that marked the transition of British society, primarily reliant on agricultural farming that then shifted toward the mechanised production of goods.

Chapter 5: Examines the importance of self-belief and focuses on reinforcing people's abilities to pursue their obligations with certainty.

Chapter 6: Examines how the ideal perspective in matters are achieved by analysing Leonardo Da Vinci's strategy that resulted in his ability to think and accomplish ahead.

Chapter 7: Evaluates the freedoms in the twenty-first century as people have been inclined to believe in what they decide to believe in. This has resulted in a trend and rise in nihilism, consumerism and the decline in religious beliefs.

Chapter 8: Introduces the strategies required in order to remain content that involves the use of the Utilitarian Third-Person Perspective tool.

Chapter 9: The representation of the individual who wants to live in balance is characterised in the life of Henry Ford. As a self-taught mechanic, Ford made the automobile affordable for the middle class through aligning his optimal goals with utilitarian objectives. The path to achieve balance is presented such that you are aligned to live in harmony.

While the strategies outlined in the contents of this book can be applied within a timely schedule within your daily life, there is also a summary of key points located at the end of each chapter. This will allow you to recall the contents for the purpose of refining your ability to achieve balance.

Balance is an objective that leads to a journey of reflection, decisions and actions toward what people perceive is right. This involves refining one's self-belief and capabilities so that they can affirm their confidence toward pursuing commitments that lead to long-term growth.

From the process of obtaining balance, you can refine your purpose of making commitments that are in alignment with your intrinsic self and society as a whole. As a result, you will face and overcome obstacles through this journey to live a fulfilled life.

In the twenty-first century, people continue to face circumstances that they are unable to control. This includes the inevitability of the changes made as a result of technological advancements and the coronavirus outbreak.

Strategies are outlined within this book that allow you to focus on what you can control, which will lead to the pursuit and completion of worthwhile objectives. Through the journey of attaining your external and internal balance, you can uphold your personal values to live at peace.

Albert Einstein once said, "A new type of thinking is essential if mankind is to survive and move toward higher levels."

The modern world has seen the increase of overall living standards due to societal and technological developments. This has led to the raising of cultural standards for people to live increasingly happy lives.

However, it is due to the availability of information that is now widely accessible, which distracts people from living a balanced life. Now, here is your opportunity to achieve harmony.

Chapter 1
What Makes You Most Happy?

People are increasingly involved with the pursuit of happiness. But what makes us happy? Smiling? That is one answer. Neurologist Isha Gupta, who specialises in headache and movement disorders, says that smiling releases dopamine and increases the level of serotonin which reduces stress.

When we are unhappy, we can choose to smile. But it is not always ideal to use seventeen of our forty-three facial muscles to sustain a lasting upward lip action. You cannot smile forever.

Instead, you can focus on the activities that scientific research has proven to keep people content in their daily lives. Since happiness is such a predominant idea for how we understand purpose in our lives, this book begins by breaking down the concept. What *is* happiness? How should it be experienced? And, is happiness a worthwhile pursuit?

There are answers to all of these questions of happiness. Harvard University undertook one of the longest studies in adult development: for eight decades, it tracked the lives of 724 men.

According to the director of the study, Professor Robert Waldinger states that harmonious relationships are what keep people happy and healthy over time.

A *Time* magazine survey in *2005* reinforces these findings. The survey asked respondents to list their major sources of happiness. Seventy-seven percent mentioned connections with their children, 76 percent listed connections with friends, 75 percent mentioned contributing to the lives of others, and 73 percent stated their relationship with their partner.

These statistics indicate that experiences such as going on holidays or purchasing goods were not found to be major sources of happiness. This is because unlike such experiences, favourable human interactions offer a sense of belonging that is pivotal to increasing a person's state of well-being.

To further decode what makes individuals happy and content, we will analyse the common predictors of happiness which involves exploring the psychology of the human mind.

Predictors of Happiness

We all experience periods when we expect to obtain greater forms of happiness. It is important to recognise which *forms* of happiness you are striving to experience.

There are two forms of happiness: *experienced utility*, which is a manifestation of an in-the-moment form of contentment and *perceived utility*, which is derived from memory-assimilated contentment. Figure 1 shows the classifications of happiness and the circumstances that inspire them.

Figure 1–Classifications of Happiness

Experienced Utility	Perceived Utility
• Connection with family, friends, colleagues, and asssociates	• Satisfaction with your standard of living
• Engaging in sports and exercise	• Satisfaction with leisure time
• Undertaking your goals and interests	• Comparisons with other people's relative enjoyment
• Sex	• Marital status
• Community participation	• Perceived home quality
	• Perceived quality of health

The experiences of different circumstances lead to different types of happiness. The types of happiness within the experienced utility category are advocated in the twenty-first century.

However, this does not indicate that it is more beneficial than perceived utility. Psychologist Daniel Kahneman states that more densely packed peak moments of experienced utility are reflective of how happy you are in the moment.

Conversely, psychologists have revealed that people perceive their experiences by their peak sentiment or by recalling the most memorable part of their experience. Essentially, people don't measure happiness by calculating the average of its different types.

The measurement is therefore, subjective and determined by a person's own inclinations. As a result, the experience of happiness is relative to each individual depending on how that person decides to measure their own experiences.

The common predictors of happiness have been published in the *Social Indicators Research* journal by professor Doh Shin and Dan Johnson, with the study including 665 household patriarchs as respondents.

The research revealed that the biggest predictor of happiness, which accounted for 30 percent of the value using the standard partial regression coefficient is determined by the degree of perceived life enjoyment *relative* to other people.

The perception of an individual's own satisfaction of their living standards and leisure time accounts for 17 percent and 16 percent of their happiness. Correspondingly, their type of marital status contributes to 16 percent, while home quality is measured at respectively 10 percent and 8 percent.

What is evident from the findings of this study is that the largest predictor of happiness is perceived life satisfaction, and that is determined not by the individual's own circumstances, but by the comparisons with other people.

This finding is emphasised by the Institute of Labour Economics in Germany, which states that the happiness gained from comparing one's income is at least twice that of the happiness gained from one's actual income.

In analysing the comparative measure to determine perceived utility, it is clear that people undertake external analysis, which indicates that this form of happiness is unreliable.

Now that the predictors of happiness have been revealed, the analysis of life satisfaction as a form of happiness will be explored to determine the optimal pursuit to strive toward.

Life Satisfaction as a Form of Happiness

A midlife crisis does not just occur among humans. According to research published by the *Proceedings of The National Academy of Sciences*, chimpanzees and orangutans also experience midlife crises.

In this study, the emotions of 508 apes were analysed by experienced zookeepers, volunteers and caretakers who knew the subjects for at least two years.

The results of this experiment show that, like humans, life satisfaction among chimpanzees and orangutans tends to decrease after adolescence until it increases again in later years.

This is known by psychologists as the U-shape curve of happiness, as represented in Figure 2, which indicates that our total life satisfaction is expected to be at its lowest levels during middle age.

Figure 2–Life Satisfaction in Relation to Age Model

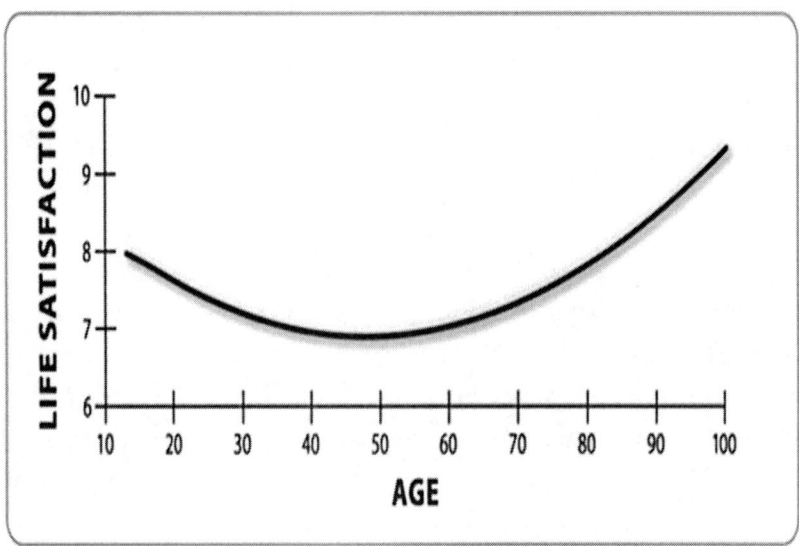

What the U-shape curve of happiness shows us is that the levels of life satisfaction are expected to change with age. This is due to different factors that affect us at each stage of our lives.

For instance, the most prominent factors causing lower levels of life satisfaction during middle age are: increased responsibilities and obligations in people's careers, relationships, financial commitments and having children.

An increase in work obligations also leads to more stress as individuals work to fulfil their responsibilities, which indicates they are less likely to spend time on activities they are interested in.

On the other end of the spectrum, people who are younger and older are not expected to undertake as many commitments. Therefore, they are more likely to experience greater levels of life satisfaction.

How we determine life satisfaction changes during our life span as it is dependent on our commitments at various stages in life.

Middle-aged group: Individuals in this group focus on their careers and relationships. Thus, they prioritise their ideal career roles, as well as finding their life partners and keeping in touch with friends, all of which requires an investment of time and energy. As a result, they will have less time for other personal interests, which makes it more difficult to attain life satisfaction.

Older populations: While the older population is expected to experience gradual decline in their energy, health and self-sufficiency, life satisfaction is predicted to increase with age.

The variables affecting perceived utility include the person's health status and family savings. Maintaining a comfortable lifestyle while having sufficient family support provides stability and reinforces well-being for this age group.

The socialising elements within the older population slowly decrease with age. Therefore, the value of relationships, particularly of close friends and family increases over time.

Furthermore, the socioeconomic comparisons also disappear, which result in the increase of life satisfaction.

Children: The quality of family life is an important factor, particularly in terms of the relationship with parents. Exercise and sports are also associated with increased levels of satisfaction and well-being within the younger age group.

Due to the internal expectations of happiness and without the means of comparisons, it is easier for children to be content in life.

The stages of a person's life present different goals from which their attainment allows them to experience the means to become satisfied. Where people strive to obtain the rewards post-goal completion, it is optimal to focus on the processes that leads to the achievement of the pursuit.

This allows people to be increasingly informed about the specific objectives that are worthy for them to pursue. The next section analyses the circumstances that affect people's ability to remain satisfied and content.

Circumstances Influencing Life Satisfaction

Life satisfaction is an indicator of happiness which is affected by a person's external environment. This section shows the extent to which social and economic factors affect your degree of life satisfaction.

'The World Happiness Report of 2022 ranked 146 countries in order of their happiness levels and revealed that life satisfaction does increase with higher income levels. However, this report also revealed that a person's life satisfaction extends beyond income to include a country's culture (in terms of relationships) and estimated life expectancy.

Let us illustrate. The Gallup World Poll in the World Happiness Report asks this question:

Evaluate your current life as a whole using the mental image of a ladder, with the best possible life for them as a 10 and worst possible as a 0.

The candidates living in high-income countries with a gross domestic product (GDP) per capita of above USD $20,000 or more answered between five and eight out of ten.

Comparatively, countries with an average GDP per capita income of USD $10,000 to USD $20,000 with the exception of Lebanon due to its currency collapse reported levels of life satisfaction between three and seven.

The analysis of such differences indicates that people living in higher income nations do not have major increases in their levels of life satisfaction relative to the alternative counterparts.

The Gallup World Poll also reveals that there are no countries with life satisfaction levels above a rating of eight. This indicates that there is a maximum limit on how satisfied people can collectively be. Therefore, instead of seeking to improve the means to increase our level of happiness, this study suggests that it is ideal to be content with what we already have.

Moreover, from analysing another poll within the World Happiness Report that focused on reporting the average life satisfaction of countries relative to their GDP per capita income shows that there are fifteen countries in Latin America that have higher levels of life satisfaction than nations in the same income bracket.

Social and economic indicators reveal that Latin America experiences high levels of income inequality, poverty and corruption. However, these fifteen nations have reported a life satisfaction level that is about ten percentage points higher than other countries with similar socioeconomic circumstances.'

This is because Latin American societies experience the positive effects of an interconnected culture. From reinforcing back to Harvard University's eight decade-long study of happiness, this reflects the importance of having harmonious relationships.

It is clear that people living in societies that are not as socioeconomically well off as others also have the capability to live happy and satisfied lives.

The Setting of Expectations

Expectations shape our desires and goals. The culture we live in today focuses on having increasingly positive life experiences. A majority of people now have freedom and equality, and we have increased our capability to obtain our needs and further our desires.

Globalisation has fostered the efficient allocation of resources, allowing us to live with access to affordable goods and services. Advancements made in technology have also increased people's quality of life by providing better access to education, health and transportation.

People of the twenty-first century have thus experienced higher living standards than those in the past. However, the consistent rise of the living standards over the last few decades has created an increase in the cultural expectations to obtain happiness.

It is important to recognise *why* people increase their expectations about seeking happiness.

A study conducted by psychology professor Andrew McLeod and Clare Conway shows that candidates who expect positive future events measure higher on the scale of personal well-being. This indicates that people that increase their expectations on their future provide positive psychological benefits including that of an optimistic outlook.

However, this is a double-edged sword as it also increases the ambition of people's goals. While higher expectations motivate individuals to accomplish their goals, if they are unable to attain these inflated goals, it will exacerbate their disappointment.

The more people expect, the less that makes them happy and the easier it will be for them to become unhappy.

If setting high standards are not ideal, people also reduce their expectations to mitigate their disappointment. Let us consider two people: Peter, who has high expectations, and Jonny, who has low expectations. Both Peter and Jonny spend their vacation on a cruise liner.

Because Peter's expectations are high, it will be easy for him to be disappointed on the trip, whether it is about relaxing on the cruise ship's deck or discovering other activities or landmarks.

On the other hand, Jonny, who has lower expectations, will be more easily satisfied with the same activities. However, Jonny will also anticipate possible ways in which things could go wrong—e.g., the boat is travelling close to rocks and may sink from a collision.

This is why, happiness cannot be shaped by changing your expectations to project different perceptions of reality. If a person adopts a lower or higher level of expectation, this will lead to the unconscious anticipation of a positive or negative future, which results in developing an unbalanced perspective toward their overall objectives.

When striving toward your commitments, set a level of expectation that is appropriate for what is predicted to occur.

To not be disappointed by your expectations of any goal, set an expectation that correlates with your present capabilities.

For example, if Michelle wants to go on a vacation overseas with her family every six months, her income must satisfy this requirement without compromising any other commitments.

If people have other financial commitments and are unable to attain this goal, they can use the setting of higher expectations as a means to motivate the actions that lead to achieving this objective.

When people are not planning or pursuing their objective, it is optimal to moderate their desire until they have established a goal that meets their requirements.

Setting the optimal level of expectation in accordance with your abilities allows you to focus on completing the task at hand. This will reduce any potential uncertainties now that you can prioritise the completion of your objectives.

Since the setting of higher or lower expectations toward happiness is not optimal, standardise the level of happiness toward the equilibrium mean. This optimal situation indicates that you do not expect to be elated or disappointed.

As a result, you can obtain the equilibrium between the expectation and the reality that will allow you to focus in the present moment.

While you are pursuing your goals, this equilibrium level of expectations will guide you to focus your energies to complete your tasks. This will increase your appreciation of the experiences in your daily life.

However, it can prove difficult for people to obtain their equilibrium mean of the expectations toward happiness and their objectives. To reinforce the ability for people to remain in the optimal state is to develop compassion.

The Phenomenology of Human Compassion

Compassion is the empathetic consciousness of a person others that furthers their ability to address difficulties. The development of compassion leads to the acceptance and approval of one's own failures and successes.

To use empathy to come to a better understanding of the self, compassion cultivates a greater sense of self-appreciation for other people. Professor Paul Gilbert stated that, "the more compassionate we are toward ourselves, the happier we are and the more resilient we become."

Through the acts of compassion, people are inclined to establish and moderate their expectations to an optimal level which will guide them to overcome adversities. This allows people to then reciprocate the acts of compassion towards providing assistance to others.

There will be times when people will dislike a task that is a part of their commitments and they inform themselves that they must endure. Through the practice of compassion, people will come to recognise that there are both positive and negative experiences in life.

It is normal not to perform proficiently in all situations because all humans have intrinsic strengths and weaknesses. Rather than focusing on such conditions, individuals are able to channel their energies toward fulfilling their commitments with compassion.

While humans all have compassionate instincts, researchers at the University of Wisconsin-Madison show that this sentiment can also be improved through honing its practice.

The steps to establish compassion include:

1. Reflecting on your past experiences and the sentiments they carry.
2. Acknowledging these sentiments through acceptance.
3. Establishing gratitude through an appreciation of experiences.
4. Recognising that you and the world are not perfect.
5. Developing resilience through being informed of truths.
6. Reciprocating acts of kindness toward others.

Through becoming more compassionate, people are then able to moderate their expectations towards optimizing their experiences.

Furthermore, instead of expecting and anticipating greater future needs, the practice of compassion promotes social connections related to increased levels of understanding, empathy, and interpersonal orientation. As a result, establishing compassion will improve your ability to assist yourself *and* others.

The psychological benefits of compassion have been explored in a research study carried out by social psychologists Elizabeth Dunn, Lara Aknin and Michael Norton.

This study shows that when candidates were given money, the individuals who spent the money on others were significantly more likely to experience an increased level of well-being compared to individuals who spent it on themselves.

Within the appropriate context, the act of giving is more pleasurable than that of receiving. This indicates that the practice of compassion toward other people benefits others and themselves.

To recognise the manner to which compassion can be optimally applied within your everyday life, requires the understanding of which objective you decide to pursue. This involves developing a comprehensive understanding of the state of happiness.

Happiness as a State of Mind

Happiness is a temporary state of mind that is defined by the experience of pleasurable emotions, ranging from contentment to intense joy. To obtain a state of happiness is to develop the manifestation of the experienced and perceived utility. This section analyses the relative state of happiness that informs you of the goals which lead to long-term fulfilment.

The twenty-first century has seen improvements in multiple components of human life, ranging from income, health, accessibility, social ability and overall living standards. Yet, according to the World Health Organisation (WHO), the level of depression has increased 18 percent worldwide from 2005 to 2015.

The main reason is that an increasing proportion of the population now perceives the value of life based on their striving toward happiness. With the improvement in modern living standards, this has resulted in the rise of people's expectations toward the experience of utility.

As a result, an increasing number of individuals now pursue greater rewards, which inadvertently reduces their focus toward the present moment. This increase in expectation toward attaining happiness is embedded in the modern culture that creates the challenge for people to live at peace.

From evaluating the presented psychological research on happiness, it is clear that individuals should focus on consistent forms to derive happiness over the long term. This includes valuing the importance of relationships, while also being satisfied with the use of leisure time and living standards.

By applying compassion within your everyday life, you can regulate your level of expectation to the equilibrium mean that allows you to experience utility without compromising the present.

This increase in self-awareness allows you to become satisfied with your life and leisure time. From valuing the importance of relationships with family, companions, friends or colleagues, you can become conscious of the inter-relational benefits, such as connectedness, belonging and well-being.

As a result, through regulating the expectations toward the equilibrium mean, you can strive to value relationships and the optimal goals as outlined in chapter 3. This will allow you to experience happiness through the process of undertaking such objectives to their completion, which leads to greater levels of self-fulfilment.

In analysing the state of happiness, there is a psychological limit as to the degree a person can be happy as explained from the findings from the World Happiness Report. While recent improvements in technology and living standards have led to the desire for greater results, this does not indicate that it is optimal for people, communities and society to increase their expectations toward obtaining happiness.

Setting higher expectations leads to the difficulty of becoming happy and is equally proportional to experiencing disappointment. As such, the pursuit of happiness is limited in its potential to consistently experience it.

The Relative State of Happiness

Do you remember a time when you were exceptionally happy? Are you able to recapture that euphoria now in this present moment?

If you cannot, you would not be alone. Many individuals experience this ineffectuality, including lottery winners. A trio of researchers at North-western University and the University of Massachusetts evaluated the well-being of twenty-two lottery winners, after they had experienced the event, were no happier than twenty-nine victims who became paraplegic or quadriplegic.

This psychology study revealed that even if the circumstances of individuals differ, once the event passes, they will experience similar levels of happiness. This is caused by what is known as hedonic adaptation that refers to the return of an equilibrium state of well-being after an emotional response from the experience of circumstances. The effect of hedonic adaptation reinforces the limitation of obtaining consistent levels of happiness.

The term *happiness* is defined as experiencing a temporary mental state of positive well-being that will inevitably appear and disappear. After experiencing happiness, the mind will inevitably return to the equilibrium mean, indicating that it is necessary for a person to then experience sadness or displeasure over a duration of time.

This is explained through the cause and effect from experiencing any emotion. For example, after experiencing consistent levels of contentment, it then becomes difficult for people to experience pleasure and it is equally proportional to become disappointed. This is represented in the Yin Yang of Figure 3 which displays the elusive changes of an emotion as shown from the arrows. The Yin represents happiness whereas the Yang represents disappointment.

Figure 3–Yin and Yang Representing the State of Happiness

The Yin and Yang exemplifies opposite forces of circumstances including those beyond the sentiment of happiness. For every good, there is bad. For every hot, there is cold. For every moment people are happy, there will also be moments when they are disappointed.

There are dots within every element as every Yin symbolised by the black has an element of Yang as shown in the white dot which is also applied vice versa.

It is clear from the psychological research and as represented by the Yin Yang that the outlined elements including the experience of happiness cannot remain constant. The changes in the experience of emotions are relative which all together result in the represented depiction of the state of balance.

In evaluating the pursuit of happiness, it is clear that striving to attain this objective is not optimal for people's state of mind. From being informed of the sentiment of happiness, this indicates that setting higher levels of expectation to achieve greater levels of in-the-moment utility is flawed.

This striving for greater experiences, such as going on repeated holidays and attaining more materialistic goods does not establish purpose, but the *temporary* state of happiness. Moreover, individuals who consistently strive to obtain happiness as a result of its experienced limits will encounter the law of diminishing returns.

This law indicates that the more a person seeks to obtain happiness, the less of a reward they will experience. Happiness is not a goal people should strive toward but rather, it is an emotion experienced from the pursuit of a desire.

The Equilibrium State of Mind

Instead of pursuing happiness, strive to attain an equilibrium state of mind. This will allow people to live in alignment with their individuality which is crucial for obtaining balance in the twenty-first century.

Living in an equilibrium state of mind directs the focus towards the present moment of whether individuals are striving toward their objectives or simply living at peace. This involves not having any preconditioned expectations about the experience of happiness.

When you are not pursuing your goals, you can live in equanimity through the moderation of your expectations. As a result, when you attain the equilibrium state of mind, it develops a well-defined purpose that is in congruence with the present.

Figure 4 shows the difference between the pursuit of happiness and the equilibrium state of mind.

Figure 4–Pursuit of Happiness and Equilibrium State of Mind

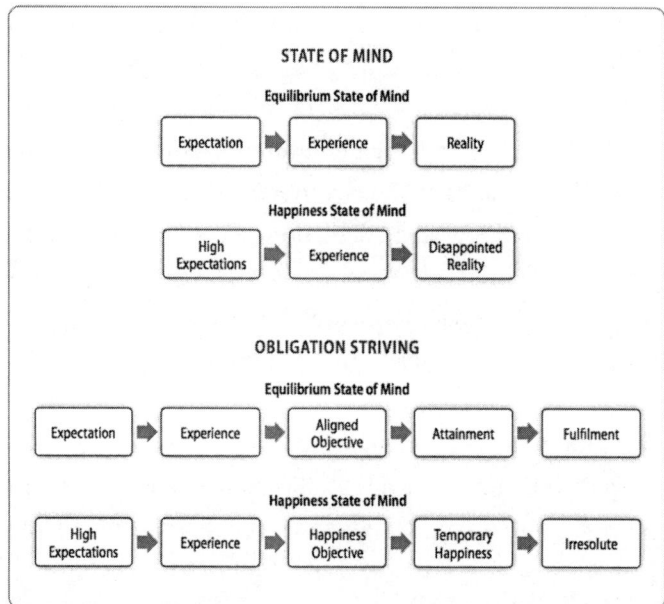

As shown from the above figure, pursuing an equilibrium state of mind is the ideal way to achieve a balanced life. It is through obtaining the equilibrium state of pursuing objectives or living in the present state that establishes the optimal expectations to attain the external and internal balance.

Key Points

1. People are involved in the pursuit of happiness in the twenty-first century.
2. The increase in modern living standards has led to raising the cultural expectation of experiencing happiness.
3. There are two forms of happiness, including *experienced* utility which is the manifestation of in-the-moment form of pleasure, and *perceived* utility which is derived from memory-assimilated contentment.
4. The biggest predictor of happiness from the research published in the Social Indicators Research by Professor Doh Shin and Dan Johnson has been revealed by people comparing the perceived life enjoyment relative to other people.
5. Director Robert Waldinger of Harvard University's eight-decade research on adult development outlines that harmonious relationships are what keep people happy and healthier throughout their lives.
6. Life satisfaction is a measure for happiness that has been revealed by psychologists as the U-shape of Happiness which predicts people at the middle-age group will experience its lowest level due to an increase in obligations and commitments.
7. What people value as important, changes throughout the course of their life and that affects how they determine their life satisfaction.
8. The Gallup Poll from the World Happiness Report reveals, there is a limit on how satisfied in life people can collectively be.
9. Analysis of the World Happiness Report reveals, there are fifteen Latin American countries that have reported higher levels of life satisfaction in comparison with nations in the same income bracket. This reinforces Harvard University's research evaluation on happiness that reflects the importance of valuing close relationships.
10. Practicing acts of compassion reinforces a person's ability to accept their experiences which establishes resilience.
11. Happiness is a temporary state of mind of positive well-being that appears and disappears over time.
12. The hedonic adaptation phenomenon explains that after experiencing any sentiment, the brain will inevitably return to the equilibrium mean.

13. The Yin Yang represents opposing elements of circumstances that results in the forming of balance.
14. There is a limit to the degree a person can be happy, which indicates that the pursuit of happiness is flawed.
15. People that obtain the equilibrium state of mind are able to live in the present moment of pursuing their goals or to be at peace.
16. This equilibrium state of mind requires not to have any preconditioned expectation toward pleasure, which allows you to live in equanimity.

Chapter 2
Social Media Renaissance

Social media is an online networking service that allows users to interact with others over the internet. Platforms such as Facebook, Twitter, Snapchat, TikTok and Instagram present another dimension of social interaction.

Instead of being limited to conventional face-to-face interactions, social media users are now able to post and upload photos and videos that allow other users to share and update content.

After engaging with other users, this online form of interaction establishes people's desire to focus on attaining external validation. The increased amount of time users spend on social media sites has developed the need to use social media proactively without experiencing its drawbacks.

History of Social Media

Social media has existed in traditional form since the Renaissance in the fourteenth century. Although the channels of communication that deliver information have changed, the spreading of social content has remained prevalent.

The Renaissance during the fourteenth to seventeenth centuries in Europe focused on the intellectual movement of reviving historical conventions in order to improve the progressiveness of the individual self.

This cultural movement toward what would be referred to as *humanism* began in Italy and the Renaissance spread throughout Western Europe.

It was during the Renaissance when the means of civic, moral and intellectual pursuits were emphasised. This led people to strive toward improving their social positioning. The invention of the printing press during the Renaissance resulted in the mass production of books that offered written knowledge, as well as communicating social news and information.

It was during this cultural shift of the Renaissance that people saw improvements in the social interactive elements within European society.

The medium of the book was utilised during the Renaissance to provide an overview of social interactions among people. Known as *alba amicorum* and translated in Latin as *book of friends*, this form of people's journal entries were filled with signatures of personalised messages and testaments of friendships.

The social element of friendship journals began in universities where students and instructors carried out the signing of signatures during graduation. The accessibility of books also increased during this period, which led to the popularity of public journals that were used among the middle, upper and aristocratic classes.

During the Renaissance period, women played an important role in the domestication of the household as their journals were used as a guest album which revealed their social circle and interests. Along with the inclusion of signatures from friends, family and acquaintances of previous household guests, these journals also contained the expression of personal interests.

The journal owners would include poems, mottos, drawings and song lyrics. As a result, the *alba amicorum* expressed people's personal values, interests and social relationships.

Public journal entries later included a career element beyond social connectivity. People working in occupations that required frequent travelling, including the role of the merchant, painter and diplomat were required to carry public journals.

Signatures of personal tributes revealed details of the relationships between the signatory and the journal holder. This form of public journal entry is similar to the modern-day résumé and career profile websites.

The modern social media platforms use the internet to allow people to connect and interact with others. Now, without any physical limitations toward engaging over social media, this has improved the manner to which people regularly communicate on a global scale.

Effect of Social Media Platforms

Today, social media provides online platforms that are an integral component for how people communicate within the twenty-first century. Social media engagements extend beyond traditional face-to-face interactions which include unique communication features.

Users on these platforms are able to reveal details of their values, interests and engagements through their social profiles. By sharing posts, uploading photos and videos, this public information lets users provide new opportunities to express themselves.

In addition to this, other features including 'like' 'love' and 'dislike' are public indicators that show the collective reception toward the shared content. As a result, people can share their own experiences beyond the expression of words using the interactive elements offered within social media applications.

The accumulation of these posts on social media will attract natural curiosity regarding the profile of each user. It is revealed from the research carried by the psychologist Leon Festinger that individuals will intrinsically make comparisons of others in order to determine their first impressions before engaging with the individual.

From making comparisons, users can recognise the collective postings of other users' profiles. Users who prioritise the value of happiness, will strive toward interacting on social media which results in a temporary heightened state of happiness.

Neuro-economist Paul Zak, working in the discipline that seeks to explain human decision-making, has revealed through his experiment of taking two blood samples ten minutes' apart after a patient commented on a Twitter post that the patient experienced a spike in oxytocin levels of 13 percent.

This change in oxytocin triggers a reward system in the brain that activates the signals responsible for social stimuli as if people are experiencing the positive social interaction in real life. This same study has also shown a decrease in the stress hormone cortisol by 11 percent, which is linked to the result of social bonding.

Other social engagement features such as tagging, sharing and following allow the user to experience varying effects of such stress hormone depending on the person's engagement with others.

Social media platforms increase the connectedness among individuals, which leads to a rise in the positive sentiments that affect people's level of happiness. The features implemented in such platforms allow users to engage with other forms of interactions beyond those of the real-life alternative.

While these individuals will experience bonding and rapport with other users, they will unconsciously compare themselves with the highlights reels of other user's profile.

From recalling chapter 1, the experience of happiness is limited, which indicates that undertaking comparisons in order to obtain perceived utility will lead to diminishing returns of the sentiment.

The accumulation of positive sentiments gained from using social media platforms leads to the desire for people to repeat the feelings associated from connectedness. Since the interactions on social media do not derive the same amount of bonding or pleasure, social media behaves as a variable reward system.

This is where the interactions made on social media, perform similar to entering the lottery or playing a game. Because people's brains are wired to seek the next reward and without being aware of its effects, they will unconsciously increase their attention on these platforms either passively through checking notifications, or by actively engaging within the social application.

Since a variable reward exists within these platforms, this is the fundamental cause as to why a large number of social media users spend an unbalanced amount of time on their phones.

Figure 5 shows the reward cycle from social media engagement and how it increases the attention toward attaining variable rewards.

Figure 5–Variable Reward Engagement Cycle

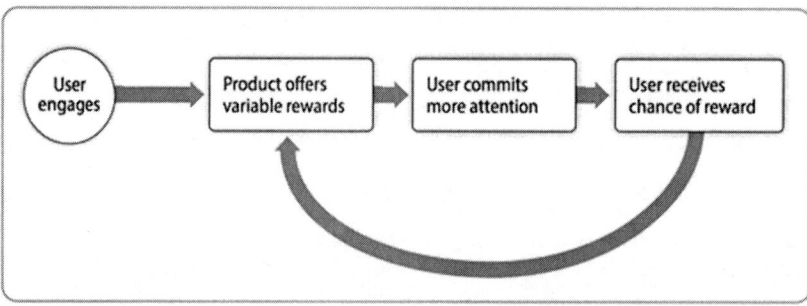

With more attention focused on these social platforms, the user experiences temporary pleasures as they engage and interact with others. However, this will also lead to an increase in their expectations of actively engaging within the services, which results in the seeking of external validation from others.

In order to not experience the inadvertent effects of using social media, it is recommended to increase your awareness of when you are engaging in activities that do not offer long-term rewards.

This can involve implementing a time or place anchor which provides reference in order to fulfil meaningful goals. As a result, people can be proactive when using social media.

While social media has its drawbacks, these platforms facilitate the seamless connection between users, which allows people to remain updated.

It is through being informed of the inadvertent effects of utilising social media that people are able to maintain the use of its services without experiencing the drawbacks.

In summary, social media allows users to interact and engage with others in another dimension using the implemented features within the applications. In addition, such platforms are a medium to identify and reinvigorate past relationships that have lapsed over time. As a result, these applications can help people engage and strengthen the value of their relationships.

On the other hand, these platforms can also be addictive as individuals who are unaware of their effects, or value the importance of happiness are prone to over-engage.

It is then optimal for people to reduce their social media use by being informed of why they use these platforms. As such, this allows users to use social media without experiencing its drawbacks.

These methods outlined that address the drawbacks of social media are effectual with a conscious mind, but it is most comprehensive to establish the equilibrium in your validation dependency.

This provides the root of the solution such that you are able to engage with others using social media and during physical interactions. From developing your own validation dependency, you are able to establish your own self-worth.

Achieving the Equilibrium of Validation

It is in human nature to seek encouragement and rapport from other individuals while also reinforcing your own internal validation. The validation obtained externally involves connecting and reciprocating through bonding within the interaction.

Since engaging with other people now requires less effort, this allows individuals to obtain greater levels of interaction online, which can result in seeking constant levels of external validation.

While seeking advice and recommendations provide other people's perspectives on matters, if individuals consistently attempt to attain the external validation without their own analysis, this reduces their ability to rely on their own perspective.

On the other hand, if an individual has established their own internal validation, it is then viable to seek other people's opinions without affecting their self-reliance.

Internally validated people reinforce their own opinions of which they are certain, and also uncertain such that from the accumulation of perspectives, they can improve their decision-making processes.

It is your own internal validation that reinforces your validation dependency. To establish your own internal validation involves reinforcing the values that underline your beliefs and perspectives.

First, the practice of self-reflection of the past informs people of their experiences about particular character traits that are beneficial, such as courage, independence and resilience. This then requires them to integrate such traits which allows them to be more comfortable with themselves.

From obtaining your own internal validation, you can reinforce your own dependency of what you are already knowledgeable and what circumstances would benefit from external opinions.

Since social media platforms connect users to obtain the perspective of others in the domains of the public feed and through personal interactions, this increases people's potential to experience positive emotions.

If people have not already developed their own validation dependency, this can lead to the temporary reward of obtaining validation through external means.

When individuals begin to rely on the opinions of others, this reduces their own self-reliance. It causes cognitive dissonance within their decision-making process.

When an individual consistently relies on the validation of others, that person will begin to experience the conflict of whether their own internal or external values hold more significance.

It is optimal to attain an equilibrium between the external and internal forms of validation in order to reinforce people's open-mindedness *and* self-sustenance.

By establishing your own internal validation, you can then take into account of the external perspectives and with your own acumen make accurate decisions.

To determine the equilibrium between applying your own external and internal validation that establishes your own self-worth, the overview of René Descartes's methodology for reasoning is presented below.

Descartes's Method of Doubt

The individual's self-worth is not to be defined by others, but what is defined by themselves.

René Descartes, regarded as the 'first modern philosopher' who abandoned traditional Aristotelian philosophy was responsible for shaping the cultural principles during the periods of the Renaissance.

By the seventeenth century, where other scholars had continued to base their cultural beliefs and theoretical principles on prior historical texts, Descartes proposed The Method of Doubt, which was intended to bring certainty to the information taught in universities and academia. This method involves:

1. Rationalising the information to be true.
2. Breaking down truths into smaller components.
3. Solving the simple problems first.
4. Making a complete list of further issues.

This method is based on the realisation that the primary mode of knowledge is discovered through the sensory experience of sight, touch, hearing, smell and taste. Descartes proposed that the previously accrued information would be subject to bias.

He believed that the lens of observation might be inaccurate as a person you saw at first glance, may often not be that person that you initially thought of and that discrepancies would also exist in the other senses.

Descartes was credited with developing the Cartesian Plane. He investigated ways to precisely position the fly and would reference its location by calculating the distance away from the walls.

Marking down this observation, he determined the fly's position to a particular point and hence developed the Cartesian Coordinate and Coordinate Plane systems.

The philosopher determined that our life is not a dream by using the rationality that because you have a conscious awareness. This indicates that people are living in their present existence.

Descartes indicated that all reliable knowledge is built up by the use of reason through logical analysis. For determining the equilibrium of an individual's validation, it is necessary to experience doubt. The process of doubt is what this philosopher describes as the origin of wisdom.

The equilibrium of validation is established through realising our external and internal needs. It is through the raising of doubt that individuals will question their own individuality.

Through reinforcing their values and beliefs, people are then inclined to develop a comprehensive awareness toward establishing their own internal validation. As a result, with this validation dependency, they are able to realise their self-worth. It is through this process of doubt that a person's self-worth is established and upheld.

Conversely, it is also through one's relationships that provide rapport and belonging which leads to an improvement of their well-being. Furthermore, the external opinions from other people are able to offer another perspective that guides individuals to make informed decisions.

As a result, this indicates that upholding one's self-worth allows people to maintain their validation dependency such that they can meet their intrinsic and external obligations.

To reinforce your own self-worth involves being informed of who you are. The next section involves analysing the degree of extraversion within one's personality trait, which allows people to align their natural inclinations with their preferred type of everyday interaction.

Extroversion, Introversion and Ambiversion

Extroversion or introversion is a central dimension of the human personality that is responsible for the degree a person is outgoing, communicative and expresses energetic behaviours.

This personality trait determines whether people draw their energies from either their internal or external environments.

Extroverts are naturally inclined to socialise in large group settings and with the availability of social media, they can further their interactions using these platforms.

Introverts, on the other hand, focus their energy inward which directs their inclinations toward engaging with smaller group interactions.

While introverts expend their energy from interacting in large social situations, extroverts gain energy over the course of these engagements. Psychologist Hans Eysenck outlined the differences between extroversion and introversion due to the varying levels of cortical arousals that the mind responds to external stimulation.

Extroverts have a naturally lower level of arousal which causes the individual to seek higher levels of external stimuli. On the other hand, introverts have a naturally high level of arousal, which leads them to avoid experiencing any further stimuli. This is the reason why introverts prefer interacting in smaller groups whereas extroverts prefer socialising in large social settings. On the social networking applications, introverts prefer to socialise on the private feeds whereas extroverts are more inclined to interact on the public domain.

There is also a third group of this human personality trait named "ambiverts" which account for the majority of the population. Consisting of a combination between the traits of both extroversion and introversion, Professor Emeritus Barry Smith at the University of Maryland states that ambiverts make up 68 percent of the population.

Ambiverts are flexible in the manner they slide up and down the extroversion to introversion scale depending on the situation. This characteristic is referred to as situational introversion which allows these individuals to become flexible and intuitive toward responding to different social settings.

For example, while attending a dinner party, the ambiverts may feel comfortable and become outgoing and talkative, whereas in a work conference, they may decide to be more inclined to learn and remain introspective rather than choosing to undertake discussions until the event has concluded.

Ambiverts are able to interact in-between listening and talking depending on whether it is in their interest to remain active or passive over the course of the interaction. The challenge for ambiverts is to recognise which side of the personality spectrum they should apply within specific situations.

The personality traits of extroverts, introverts and ambiverts all manifest different levels of cortical arousal that motivates particular forms of actions to which they are naturally inclined toward.

Figure 6 shows the extraversion to introversion personality scale of where people are naturally stimulated.

Figure 6–Personality Traits of Extroversion, Ambiversion and Introversion

Personality Trait	Extrovert	Ambivert	Introvert
Sociability	Prefers to connect with other people	Periodically seeks out other people	Prefers to connect in smaller groups
Activity	Prefers to be physically active	Moderation of level of activity	Prefers to remain in one place
Amicability	Expresses positive feelings	Articulates a degree of positive feelings	Reserved in expressing feelings
Expressiveness	Expresses with regard for reactivity	Expresses moderate care in personal expression	Expresses with the discretion of reactivity
Assertiveness	Desires for the inclination to lead	Accepts responsibility to lead others	Prefers to be independently passive
Pleasure Seeking	Desires to interact in large groups and in outside environment	Seeks moderation between interacting in large and smaller groups	Desires to engage in small groups of interaction or seeks to be alone

The traits of the extroversion to introversion affects the manner to which a person is naturally inclined to be sociable, active, amicable, expressive, assertive and seek pleasure.

These components are not restricted to remain constant within a person's personality trait.

Whether you are an introvert, extrovert or ambivert, you are able to commit to establishing character traits from the other side of this personality spectrum.

This is revealed by clinical psychologist Doctor Joshua Klaplow, stating that introverts are able to show extroverted traits within the manner they interact. However, they may experience a fallback to their original trait if they are anxious or exhausted.

People would benefit from establishing traits from the other end of this personality spectrum when it is beneficial for them to fulfil their internal or external needs.

For example, Henry is an extrovert and their job requires them to spend time travelling alone, and he also interacts in one-on-one settings with his clients, it is optimal to apply the traits of introversion.

Conversely, Sarah is an introvert and in her surfing supervision role requires her to teach and lead in large group settings, it is optimal to utilise extroverted traits during such circumstances.

To have both traits of introversion and extroversion will increase your ability to be flexible when interacting with different people and circumstances.

By being informed of this dimension of your personality, you can improve your competency to fulfil your internal and external obligations.

As a result, you can further the knowledge of your personality that reinforces the value of your self-worth. It is through recognising your own personal values and abilities that leads to attaining the internal balance.

Key Points

1. Social media existed during the Renaissance in a journal format that had been used to publicly display people's interests, social connections and career commitments.
2. The modern social media platforms allow users to extend beyond traditional face-to-face interactions whereby people are able to connect seamlessly.
3. Each platform has their own features including posting likes, dislikes, tagging and sharing, which allow their users to interact in experiences beyond the expression of words.
4. Social media platforms allow users to strengthen relationships while also identifying and reinvigorating past relationships that have lapsed over time.
5. As users engage using social media platforms, they will attract the inclination to make first impressions toward other people. Psychologist Leon Festinger reveals that people will naturally make comparisons before engaging with the other person.
6. Research carried by neuro-economist Paul Zak has revealed that social media engagements result in social stimuli that are reciprocal to the experiences of the social interactions in real life.
7. The accumulation of positive experiences gained using social media platforms function as a variable reward engagement cycle.
8. Social media offers both benefits and drawbacks depending upon how the user decides to interact with these services, whether as a means of connectivity or entertainment.
9. In order for people to not experience the inadvertent effects of social media, they can direct their focus to pursue long-term goals and establish an internal validation.
10. The equilibrium of validation involves upholding your own self-worth while maintaining your validation dependency.
11. To experience doubt is regarded by René Descartes as the origin of wisdom.
12. Our society consists of extroverts, introverts and with a majority of the population being ambiverts.

13. Extroverts have a lower level of cortical arousal whereas introverts have a higher level of arousal, which results in the difference to how people are naturally stimulated to act.
14. It is viable for people to obtain another dimension of extroversion or introversion which can refine their capabilities to fulfil their obligations.
15. To further your self-awareness as explored in chapter 3, you can pursue the optimal goal that aligns your individual traits with the external opportunities to obtain self-fulfilment.

Chapter 3
The Optimal Goal Strategy

To be yourself in a world that is constantly trying to make you something else is the greatest accomplishment.
—Ralph Waldo Emerson

Napoleon Bonaparte, a military general and first emperor of France, inherited the French Revolution that spread the principles of liberty, equality and fraternity throughout Europe.

Although Napoleon was born into minor nobility from the island in Corsica, his family was of Italian descent, which made it challenging for him to interact within French society. The eighteenth-century French empire had initially operated under a feudal system before the French Revolution.

This meant that the existing king, Louis XVI, would grant land to the noblemen who would in turn receive services from knights, merchants and farmers. The absolute monarch experienced administrative inefficiencies that raised the inequality between the rich and poor classes.

For Napoleon to be considered a French aristocrat, he had to overcome the odds in both military and political avenues in order to re-establish the prosperity for the common citizens of French society.

At the age of twenty-four, Napoleon was exiled from his homeland of Corsica where they had considered him a traitor due to losing a battle with the Paoli army that strived to maintain Corsican independence from France.

Napoleon left his homeland and travelled across the Mediterranean Sea to France. Despite his unconventional origins and initial exile from Corsican society, Napoleon utilised his strengths, interests and opportunities to rise to power.

The struggles and successes of Napoleon Bonaparte and other significant figures are mentioned here to shine light on the strategies outlined in this chapter.

It is integral to have self-awareness of your temperament, and abilities in order to recognise which objectives are worthwhile to undertake.

Through this, you can pursue the optimal goals that will result in satisfying your intrinsic aspirations and external commitments.

Enrolled in the college of Brienne in France, Napoleon left home at the age of eight and began his military education. Having spoken French in a heavy Corsican accent, Napoleon was ridiculed by many of his classmates.

During Napoleon's early education, his father's health deteriorated due to stomach cancer, which made his family subject to poverty. Relying on his scholarship to financially survive, Napoleon excelled in the fields of mathematics, geography and history.

These disciplines of study later guided him to his admission into the military academy. Since Napoleon was born from an island, he was pressured by the then-governor of Corsica, Count Marbuef, to apply for a position in the navy. This application was rejected.

Napoleon continued to excel in mathematics and geography, where he strived to utilise his strengths, and he enrolled in the artillery branch of the military. His admission was successful and this decision proved pivotal in forming future opportunities in his career prospects.

After he left Corsica, his first military campaign fighting for the French Revolution demonstrated his proficiencies during the Siege of Toulon. Napoleon, at age twenty-four, planned the successful recapture of the port and he was awarded the rank of brigadier general from artillery commander.

The soldiers hesitated to undertake Napoleon's plan with precise execution until General Jacques Dugommier arrived to confirm that his plan was the only viable option. Despite his victory in this campaign, it remained uncommon for any candidate being a French commander to rise to such position. Napoleon, would aim to utilise his position to transform his reputation on his return to Paris.

Napoleon frequented the salons, which were gatherings hosted by prominent women of French Society and where literature and intellectual ideas were discussed. Although he held a high military rank, the noble class did not accept Napoleon and treated him no better than any other ambitious solider.

Alone and isolated, Napoleon focused on furthering his aspirations. He was given an opportunity to prove himself when thousands of the monarch's supporters marched into Paris with the aim of toppling the Republican Government.

Being known for his military capabilities at the Battle of Toulon as a result of his artillery capabilities, the Republican Government gave Napoleon the command to repel the attack. Cannon were used to counter the monarch-advocating mobs and their defeat earned Napoleon unprecedented popularity and the patronage from the new government.

Innate Potential

We are all born in a time where equality has become increasingly widespread. Men and women rights are equally defined while discrimination is considered prejudice. This raises the question of why do certain people accomplish more than others?

Natural intelligence and favourable upbringing opportunities are among the common answers. Yet this answer lies from the selection of what is optimal for each person to strive toward.

Positive psychology is a field that involves the scientific study of what makes life worth living. Dr Martin Seligman, a founder of positive psychology stated that people must recognise and use their strengths for a greater purpose than themselves in order to live content and meaningful lives.

This implies that individuals are required to recognise their strengths and moral values. Focusing on your strengths allows you to perform tasks with the proficiency to obtain high level of work satisfaction which results in a positive feedback loop.

The Gallop Report shows that out of 530 teams, the managers who received feedback associated with their strengths increased their productivity by 13 percent compared with managers who did not receive any positive response.

Correspondingly, when people recognise their weaknesses, this awareness informs them of when they will face challenging situations that require additional effort to overcome.

Since our minds are hardwired to behave in the manner we are naturally inclined toward, this indicates that it is not worthwhile for people to consistently work alongside their weakness.

In the cases where it is necessary for people to apply their weaknesses, they can fulfil these tasks by concentrating on pivoting their naturally inclined propensities towards completing their obligations.

Nevertheless, it is from one's motivation to refine their strengths that leads them to increase their abilities and fulfil their objectives.

From the opportunity cost of choosing a person's strength over their weaknesses as reflected by Napoleon Bonaparte's career advancements, it is clear that focusing on where one's strengths lie is advantageous towards achieving their goals.

To work alongside your strengths in your career field improves the opportunity to fulfil the tasks with proficiency such that you can direct your focus toward your other desired goals.

For people to be informed of their proficiencies allows them to optimise the use of their strengths and weaknesses on a daily basis. Aligning one's strengths with their commitments forms the efficiency which allows them to fulfil their obligations.

When it is unavoidable for people to utilise their weaknesses, they can fulfil these tasks by directly focusing on making the improvements. For example, Sarah is a financial analyst who is required to analyse consumer data but is starting to lose job satisfaction so she intends to change to the role of strategic business planning.

Since both current and future roles require data analytics, refining this weakness will improve her abilities to reach such objective.

Correspondingly, it is optimal for people to utilise their strengths to complete their objectives where it is viable. The rewards of working with one's strengths over an alternative option include completing their tasks with efficiency such that people are able to obtain greater levels of fulfilment.

People's time and energy are limited, and therefore, it is optimal to accomplish tasks with proficiency such that they can meet their other obligations. As such, people using their strengths increase their ability to further their potential.

There are obligations that align with your strengths, however, some of these pursuits do not result in any long-term growth. The Optimal Goal Strategy allows you to use your strengths toward pursuing the goals that furthers your fulfilment and self-worth.

As a result, this will lead to satisfaction from accomplishing your tasks with proficiency, while also providing value to the greater society.

The Optimal Goal

Very few people come into this life with complete awareness of what they are born to do. To develop accurate goals is an essential component that directs you toward the trajectory of where you intend to experience success.

The optimal goal involves combining your strengths, intrinsic habits and the value you offer to society that aligns your personal traits with external opportunities.

To pursue the optimal goal allows people to use their own natural abilities to accomplish the obligations in society that will result in self-fulfilment.

While many of the objectives that individuals aspire to fulfil may not be accomplished, these goals contain knowledge that is valuable for being informed of what is worth pursuing. It is from a person's previous pursuits that determine whether they have an interest toward the process in order to fulfil their objectives.

To self-reflect toward one's previous objectives informs people of not only whether they experienced contentment from the process, but also, it provides knowledge of their strengths and weaknesses.

Through this process of contemplation, you can further obtain knowledge of your strengths and the processes that lead toward developing your optimal goal.

Our minds are naturally inclined toward particular thoughts that over time result in the development of new interests. This is particularly evident during periods when you procrastinate and decide to deviate from the present task toward other thoughts.

Through being aware of these cases of procrastination, people are able to be informed of the matters that your mind has a natural tendency toward. These habits of thought may coincide with your strengths, interests or passions.

The thoughts that your mind has a natural tendency toward, are an essential component of your personal traits that will result in forming your optimal goal.

The value you offer to society is explained by what benefits your activity contributes to other people or the world as a whole. This does not need to be carried only through altruistic or philanthropic actions, but rather, takes into account what people have provided that has been of service.

This may be derived from your career, where you may contribute by providing financial and home loan services that help customers receive the necessary support to meet their needs.

Alternatively, people may also pursue interests that can include solving a lifestyle problem, such as designing an adjustable back chair that helps others sit with an optimal posture that prevents back pain.

Whether it is through your career or interests, it is necessary to recognise what value you contribute to society.

To obtain optimal goal requires you to work alongside their strengths, while having a cognitive interest, and ensure that it offers value to society. This is shown in Figure 7 where the optimal goal aligns toward a person's passion, opportunity and aspiration.

Figure 7–Optimal Goal Strategy

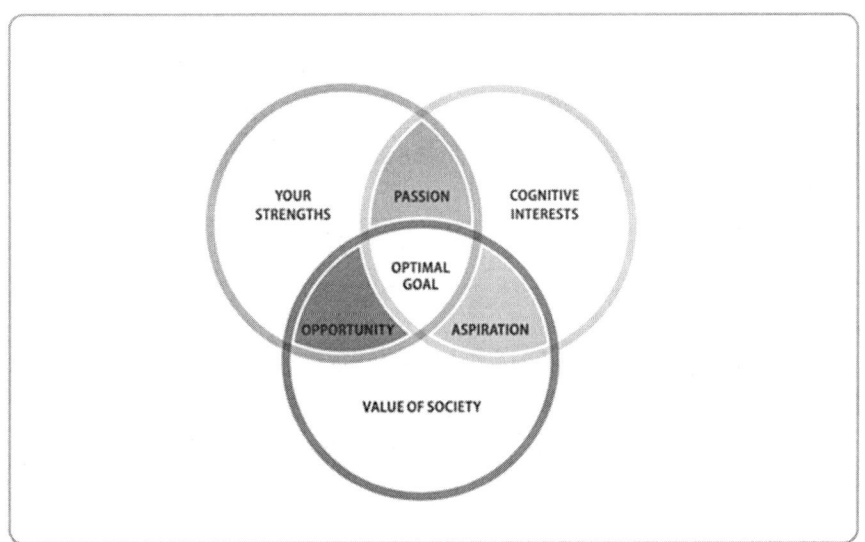

The key attributes of the Optimal Goal Strategy consist of people's aspirations, opportunities and passions. For one's cognitive interest to coincide with the value of society, people will develop aspirations that can also benefit others.

Correspondingly, a person's passion is determined through the alignment of their thoughts and strengths. The opportunities presented in society are determined by aligning one's strengths with the needs that are valued in society. It is from the combination of these attributes that determines the optimal goal.

Our work is the activity that accounts for most of our time in our adult life with the exception of sleep. Many people's careers are determined based on their ability to work alongside their strengths, based from their passion or deciding if there is value perceived by society.

The requirement of work, is to obtain tangible and intangible rewards, such that people are able to obtain sufficient resources to fulfil their other life commitments. This involves analysing whether the work environment is amicable, provides job satisfaction and sufficient financial compensation. Through pursuing the optimal goal, people can obtain life satisfaction that revitalises other areas in their lives.

The optimal goal provides value to society, while aligning people's strength of which allows them to obtain financially compensation and recognition.

This will increase one's ability to choose which jobs offer adequate intangible rewards, whether it is to choose a favourable working environment or to have job satisfaction.

Work-life balance is commonly used as a term where people are able to obtain their work and personal commitments in an equitable manner.

Through obtaining tangible and intangible rewards from work, this will refine people's ability to achieve their work-life balance.

In the cases where people are currently unable to pursue their optimal goal due to existing commitments, they can use their present career and experience as leverage for when an ideal opportunity comes along.

This may require pursuing a similar role or furthering their knowledge or education. By positioning themselves for a future opportunity, people can attain an optimal goal of experiencing self-fulfilment by aligning their traits with the value they provide to society.

Through pursuing the optimal goal, you will experience a positive reward system of satisfying your internal traits and external commitments. This can be applied to furthering your career or finding new interests.

When people apply their optimal goal within their job, they can optimise obtaining tangible and intangible rewards. And from obtaining satisfaction from their work, individuals are then able to focus on the other areas in their life that they are inclined towards.

As a result, pursuing optimal goals will allow you to align your intrinsic traits with providing value to society so that you can achieve your work-life balance.

The Equilibrium of Pursuit

One of the fundamental objectives in life is to be self-aware so that people can align their individuality with their goals. To fulfil the internal aspirations is an essential quality that reinforces people's ability to recognise which objectives are worthwhile to accomplish.

It is through being aware of a person's own obligations that they can obtain the clarity of which goals are worthy of struggle. People that are comprehensively aware of their own innate qualities can make the ideal course of action in an equitable manner.

Nikola Tesla, born in 1856, was an engineer responsible for designing the alternating-current electric system, which remains the predominant electrical system used in modern society.

As a student, Nikola displayed a talent in solving mathematical problems that soon became an obsession. His talented abilities in this subject led to his teachers suspecting and consequently accusing him of cheating.

It later turned out that he had memorized the entire logarithm within his memory. By the age of nineteen, Nikola was accepted at Polytechnic Institute for their electrical engineering course.

During his university tenure, he became engaged in an ongoing debate with a professor over the perceived flaws of direct-current motors. Tesla stated that he would demonstrate how the electromagnetic field of a motor could better maintain the flow of electricity.

He developed an intrinsic passion to solve this question and considered it, "a question of life and death." Tesla spent six years working on the project while neglecting his own well-being. This led to one of his several nervous breakdowns throughout his life.

The obsession of finding improvements to the direct-current electrical motors led to a loss of motivation for his university studies and work.

This led to the decline in his psychological state as he became addicted to gambling and lost his tertiary tuition money. This resulted in his subsequent disenrollment from university.

After he moved to Budapest while recovering from a nervous breakdown, he was walking across a public park when he saw a 'vision.' He captured it through a drawing that depicts a rotating magnetic field with several alternating electricity currents.

It was from this realisation that he perceived a new method to the direct-current electrical motor. Up to this point in time, the direct-current worked with a magnetic field and remained constant as an electric current flowed in one direction.

Tesla's discovery of the alternating current changed the flow of the electric current by adding a stator in the motor that proved to be effective in sending electricity over long distances.

Not only was it easier to change the voltage for the transmission and distribution of an alternating-current system than using direct current, electricity plants and transmission costs were also cheaper to build and operate.

Tesla then designed and patented the alternating-current motors and associated power systems that are used in electricity grids to this day.

This innovation at the time improved the spread of electrical efficiency in many households. Nikola held more than 300 patents throughout his life. However, it was because of his unbalanced dedication toward scientific pursuits that led to the experience of his many downfalls in life.

He experienced nervous breakdowns and went bankrupt during his later years. The innovator remained disinterested in any other passion with the exception of dedicating his time to science.

Although it is important for people to recognise their strengths, this does not indicate that it is optimal to devote their life to focusing on one pursuit. The strategy to live optimally is to pursue commitments that are in alignment with one's own internal aspirations and externals needs.

To accomplish this, people will need to optimise the opportunity cost of their pursuits while maintaining their own state of well-being. It is through one's own experiences that they can refine their decision-making processes which leads to the growth of their personal development.

In evaluating Nikola Tesla, he remained persistent toward following his strengths in the fields of science and discovered multiple innovations including the AC induction motor. However, this approach of pursuit striving was at the expense of establishing an academic pathway that would have reinforced the stability of his well-being.

If Tesla had pursued his obligations in an equitable manner after attaining self-awareness, he could have focused on completing his electrical engineering degree. As a result, he could have pursued a career relating to this passion, which would have allowed him to remain financially stable to undertake his scientific experiments.

It is through obtaining an equilibrium state of mind that guides people to pursue their objectives with reasonable expectations. This will further people's ability to fulfil their internal and external objectives in a balanced manner.

The greatest thing in the world is to know how to belong to oneself.

—Michel de Montaigne

Strategies of Self-Awareness

Many people's understanding of themselves comes from existing positions of what they perceive in themselves. However, it is difficult for individuals to realise how to achieve their own potential without realising the traits that define their individuality.

This requires attaining self-awareness which involves undertaking their own personal reflections in order to further the realisation of their individuality.

The following steps establish and refines your self-awareness.

1. Where do You Spend Your Time?

The initial perception and analysis of your thoughts determines the actions you have undertaken. Recall the periods of time when you decided to choose a particular activity over an alternative.

While this may be perceived as a natural course of action, it is also driven by your unconscious perceptions. For example, you may prefer to going to the same cafe with regular friends that you frequently visit rather than exploring other coffee places and meet new people.

Reflecting on the reasons behind determining a course of action provides an unconscious insight of the personality traits that drive your action.

Beyond the degree to which a person is open within one's personality includes their agreeableness, conscientiousness, extroversion and neuroticism, which are known as the Big Five personality traits.

Neuroticism refers to how a person deals with their emotions and stress. On the other hand, conscientiousness refers to the degree they are aware of the consequences of their behaviour and that affects the degree to which a person is organised and exercises self-control. It is from these personality traits that psychologists explain consistencies in people's actions.

Where you spend your time outlines the personality traits that influence the degree that it has determined your action. Through reflecting on your past experiences and deliberating on the reasons behind the course of action you had undertaken, you are able to further your self-awareness.

As a result, this will enhance the realisation of your personality and personal aspirations.

2. What Are Your Natural Inclinations?

Recognising your natural inclinations provides an insight to the possible areas where you are able to direct your attention. This involves being aware of your strengths and personal interests, which allows you to undertake the pursuits and rewards you intend to experience.

To have an interest in an objective while working with your strengths results in a positive reward cycle of intrinsic rewards and external recognition. However, this can lead to an excess in the time spent on the passion as evident from evaluating the case of Nikola Tesla.

It is important to balance your natural inclinations by pursuing your objectives while also fulfilling your personal obligations. This way, you do not experience excess stress, fatigue and anxiety that can result in burning out from work. To achieve this equanimity between a person's internal and external goal strivings benefits from personal self-care.

Figure 8–Personal Attributes of Self-Care

Physical	Emotional	Social	Intrinsic
This includes sleep, exercise, walking, physical releases, eating healthy and rest.	This involves emotional recognition and regulation. For managing stress, utilise the practice of compassion.	This includes undertaking social interactions and personal engagements to reciprocate rapport and belonging.	This involves connecting with your innate needs and desires. Spending time with yourself will give you the capability to reflect and regulate your thoughts and sentiments.

People that recognise their natural inclinations with the exercise of self-care are able to uphold the state of their well-being. This will allow them to pursue their internal and external objectives in an equitable manner, of which will reinforce their individuality.

3. What Goals Are Worth Your Struggle?

From the pursuit of your prior objectives and optimal goals, you are able to recognise the processes that you determined are worthwhile to overcome. From persevering over adversity, you are able to be informed of the intrinsic value and rewards of accomplishing your commitments.

Ludwig van Beethoven was a composer for classical music who was regarded by his teachers to be hopeless in his composing abilities. In addition, he was diagnosed with deafness at the age of twenty-six.

Despite this, he composed music and, at the pinnacle of his career, he produced many of his most renowned works. Beethoven stated that, "music comes to me more readily than words" which is reflective of the enthusiasm toward the field of art.

He composed music using his memory attributed to recalling the sound of the instruments and using bone-conduction hearing aids.

To accomplish challenging objectives, whether it is in your career, education or relationships, this provides an awareness of the processes and rewards you are motivated toward.

By analysing the adversities of your previous experiences, you can further the awareness of your own individuality. As a result, this will establish clarity for any future pursuits you perceive are worth pursuing.

4. Further Your Awareness from External Sources

To obtain additional self-awareness knowledge, the perspectives from reliable people can provide new insights and clarity on your individuality.

There are times where there are unconscious actions which you are not comprehensively informed about. Such discussions provide insights toward your unconscious inclinations that can reveal further information regarding your personality traits and natural tendencies. This will allow you to obtain external view-points, that from your own deliberation, you are able to further enhance your self-awareness.

5. Who Do You Aspire to Become?

Throughout people's life, they will have contemplated who they aspired to become. The process of reflecting behind the reasons of this ambition can provide further insights into one's personality traits, values and objectives. It is through determining the intentions of your ambitions which allows you to obtain further awareness of your individuality.

Benefits of Self-Awareness

Self-awareness provides essential knowledge that reinforces people's personality and actions that underline their character. Individuals that align their personality traits with the objectives that they are willing to face difficulty toward is representative of the commitments they are inclined to accomplish.

Through refining your self-awareness, this reduces the decisional uncertainties in your life, which will refine your ability to accomplish commitments and interact with increased confidence in your relationships.

Correspondingly, there are individuals who avoid the need to obtain self-awareness. However, it is through not being aware of their own personality and character that leads to the raising of doubts.

It is from obtaining self-awareness that people can embrace their own individuality. As a result, they are then able to align their decisions with the external objectives which results in self-fulfilment.

Going Backwards Before Going Forward

There are periods in human history where it was necessary for civilisation to experience a backward trend. The society and the individual human alike require us to take a step back before we are able to proceed forward.

It is during these periods of time where people are required to consolidate their self-awareness and personal values. This process allows people to then pursue goals that lead to self-fulfilment. Each individual forms the collective of people that altogether contribute to the shaping of society.

The upkeep for peace was a struggle throughout European civilisation during the Dark Ages in the medieval period. Marked by the fall of the last Western Roman Emperor, Romulus Augustus, in 476 AD, this was a time where urban life in the cities became increasingly non-existent.

This represented a period where the quality of life for the Roman citizens began to experience a decline as the acquiring of resources, food and safety were questioned with doubt.

The Roman Empire during the fifth century AD experienced various external issues, including ongoing barbaric invasions and the administrative challenges caused by overexpansion.

To mitigate administrative issues, the Roman Empire was split between the East and West with the respective capitals of Milan and Constantinople. Having failed to assemble enough troops to defend the frontiers of the empire, the Romans began to rely on hiring mercenaries.

While forming peace with the Visigoth tribe, Roman officials forced the starving Goths into trading their children into slavery. Internal issues in the state became increasingly prevalent due to a shortage of and overreliance on slaves, as the conquests of Roman expansion halted in the second century.

In addition to this, political instability fuelled by corruption and incompetence in the Roman senate led to the loss of trust among many of its citizens. The loss of virtues, moral principles and mutual respect were the fundamental causes responsible for the decline of the Western Roman Empire.

The fall of the Roman Empire led to centuries of instability throughout Europe as regional lords, kings and later Vikings fought to gain power. Due to the instability, regular citizens had left their fields unfarmed as resources had become scarce.

This was exacerbated with the collapse of the Roman trade networks where the existing infrastructure including roads, bridges, aqueducts and sewer mains became neglected to the state of disrepair.

From the ongoing battles and conflicts over the next few centuries, this period was marked by instability as many people were subject to starvation and poverty.

The First Crusade in 1095 was the turning point, as the sovereignties that held Christian beliefs formed an alliance for a common purpose of taking back the city of Jerusalem. Internal battles that had continued for centuries were ended as kings and lords combined to join forces for such conquest.

It took six centuries after the fall of the Western Roman Empire until Europe was reunited for a common purpose of the First Crusade. This then led to the development of the Renaissance, which led to a focus toward the disciplines of technology, sciences and cultural progression.

The loss of values during the end of the Western Roman Empire caused a period of instability only for civilisation to advance thereafter.

In the twenty-first century, many people that perceive the importance of their desires will hinder their own inclination to take a step back. However, the people who have attained self-awareness are able to pursue the external goals that results in their personal accomplishment.

Attaining self-awareness and pursuing the optimal goal strategy leads to the progress made to achieve the internal and external balance.

Key Points

1. Self-awareness is the recognition of a person's character traits that bring clarity to their individual uniqueness.
2. It is through attaining self-awareness that people are able to have focus on achieving the commitments that are worthwhile to them.
3. Despite the struggles Napoleon Bonaparte faced, he utilised his strengths as an artillery commander and that resulted in the rise in his rank. His opportunities then led him to re-establish prosperity for common French citizens.
4. In the field of positive psychology, Dr Martin Seligman states that a person must recognise and utilise their strengths for a greater purpose than themselves in order to live a content and meaningful life.
5. It is effective for people to utilise their strengths over their weaknesses from the context of undertaking an opportunity cost.
6. The optimal goal requires people to work with their strengths and have a cognitive interest, which provides value to society.
7. When people are unable to pursue their optimal goal due to existing obligations, they can utilise their existing career skills and experience to position themselves when new opportunities become available.
8. Nikola Tesla pursued his commitments that were in alignment with his strengths. While he would discover multiple innovations including the alternating-current electricity system, this was at the compromise of his well-being.
9. The strategies to obtain self-awareness include using the Five-Factor model to be informed of their personality trait, following their natural inclinations, furthering their awareness from external sources and recognising who they aspire to become.
10. By obtaining self-awareness people are able to be comprehensively informed of who they are, which brings clarity to their decision-making and the objectives they aspire to accomplish.
11. People that accept their individuality are able to show gratitude to themselves and others, which leads to improvements in their relationships.
12. It is in human nature for people and society alike to experience setbacks before proceeding forward.

Chapter 4
The Balance of Change

Our environment constantly challenges us with opportunities to grow. The first industrial revolution marked the transition of British society that was primarily reliant on agricultural farming, which shifted to the production of goods and provision of services.

It was from the improvement of agricultural cultivation methods and the invention of the steam engine that led to the transition of the first industrialisation. This period is reflective of the twenty-first century as changes are becoming increasingly prevalent and people are faced with the same question of whether to embrace or neglect change.

These decisions will impact people's jobs, interests and commitments. Through recognising the stages of change and by undertaking the informed change analysis, you can capitalise on the transitions made in the twenty-first century.

The First Industrial Revolution

Beginning in Britain from the 1760s, the first industrial revolution was responsible for the transition away from agricultural reliance to a manufacturing-based society. It was during this period that Britain experienced a shift toward industry-based goods and consumerism, while new and improved farming methods, such as crop rotation produced a sufficient food supply for the population.

This encouraged many citizens to leave their farms and migrate to cities and factories for higher wages. Although the first phase of industrialisation was marked by labour exploitation of this vulnerable section of society, it was a fundamental period responsible for improvements in the transportation, mining and textile industries that helped shape society to the present day.

The emergence of railroads facilitated the progress of industrialisation through the transportation of energy resources and the production of goods. Steam-powered trains that relied on coal as a power source were tasked with transferring coal deposits throughout Britain.

Accessibility of these coal supplies and the ease of railroad transportation to carry large loads enabled the smelting of iron, which was a crucial resource in the production of rail lines, water pipes, bridges, machinery and ships. The use of these new energy sources improved the transportation and quality of goods accessible for its citizens.

The textile industry was one of the primary industries of employment during the first phase of industrialisation and it experienced changes in the production of material goods.

New inventions such as the Spinning Jenny and the Water Frame reduced the time required to produce woollen and cotton goods.

Prior to the industrial revolution, clothes were produced from the cottage industry and were knitted from the citizen's home and sold to the merchants. However, the challenge in the cottage industry was that there was not enough thread for the cloth sewer due to inefficiencies of threading from the available technologies.

The Spinning Jenny was developed during the industrial era and this machine improved thread production: it was able to sew eight threads at once, rather than one. In addition to this, the Water Frame was invented to stretch out the cotton with greater strength before twisting it, which used water power harnessed from river currents, producing stronger quality threaded materials.

These technologies, together with the steam engine, led to the development of steam-powered cotton mills that threaded and wove cloth in a mechanised process using machinery rather than manual labour.

As the process for the production of clothing and textile goods became more efficient and reliable, this resulted in the production of cheaper goods made in large quantities.

The construction and shipbuilding industries also flourished during the first industrialisation. The production of iron, nails and glass also led to the developmental improvements in bridges, buildings and steamship designs.

Merchant ships then improved along with the technological advancements, which resulted in faster and more reliable sea travel for the British population.

There are both benefits and drawbacks to the transition into industrialisation. Drawbacks during the initial stage of the industrial revolution included poor working conditions, particularly among unskilled laborers.

With the improvement of agricultural practices leading to the increased supply in yield, less labour was required in this field. This was similarly the case for people working in the cottage industry where technology including the water frame and steam-powered cottage mills would improve the production of clothing.

The improvement of technological processes promoted efficiency in the production of goods but at the expense of reducing the need for previous labour processes. As a result, a large proportion of the British population working in such industries had to move to the cities and work in industries that provided the incentive of higher wages.

The first phase of industrialisation also offered new opportunities in industries, including skilled labour in railroads, maritime, agriculture and metal works. Towns and cities were urbanised and offered a more efficient utilisation of resources.

Trade, infrastructure, businesses and government administration also functioned in a more effective manner than during the period prior to the first industrialisation of many small village populations.

Moreover, the industrial revolution allowed an individual to accrue wealth through better opportunities for work that led to a rise in their social class. This resulted in the emergence of the middle class.

These occupations included shopkeepers, accountants, lawyers, clerks, managers, engineers, skilled laborers and public servants. Real wages in that period also rose as a larger quantity of goods and services became increasingly available.

Trade during the industrial era also increased, which enabled access to foreign agricultural crops, food and textile products. As a result, the quality of life improved for a majority of the people living in the first industrialisation, and it was specifically evident for individuals who had embraced change.

While the working conditions of unskilled labour remained unfavourable, people living pre-industrialisation experienced greater hardships, as they had to cultivate their own crops and manually produce their own household goods.

In addition to this, a majority of individuals working before the industrial revolution were reliant on the seasonal employment of crop cultivation rather than receiving fixed incomes. This meant that most individuals living during that period had to prepare food supplies for the remaining months of the year.

Working in a factory provided workers with housing estates that were initially subject to unfavourable living conditions. However, such working conditions later improved with legislative changes. This progressive movement for equitable working-class rights and labour laws continued throughout later centuries.

Nevertheless, the integration of machinery in the production of goods reduced the amount of strenuous labour that was required.

It also promoted efficiency in the production process such that the goods and services became more widely accessible for all citizens.

New opportunities from the emergence of the middle class enabled people to live a better quality of life compared to the restrictive nature of the agricultural cottage-based period. For individuals living in the period of the first industrialisation, there were many favourable outcomes for those who were inclined to embrace change.

Conversely, people who were reluctant to transition to the then-emerging circumstances experienced setbacks. This is similarly reflective in the twenty-first century where many technological advancements have improved the production of goods and provision of services.

From the analysis of the first industrialisation, it is clear there were people who benefited from the changes, while others experienced setbacks.

To benefit from the changes in the twenty-first century involves carrying out an Informed Change Analysis that determines whether the change is worthwhile for people to undertake.

Informed Change Analysis

While not all forms of change are beneficial, it is important to be receptive to new perspectives and circumstances. The informed change analysis investigates the external commitments that are required to be carried out for the person while also including their internal traits to determine which circumstances are most appropriate.

Undertaking this strategy requires carrying out an impartial stance to improve the receptivity toward all perspectives of the analysis components. This will allow people to make an evaluation as to whether the change is worthwhile to carry out.

Steps Of the Informed Change Analysis

1. Collect Past and Present Information Relating to the Specific Field. The comprehensiveness of the information required is determined by the extent of the effect of the possible change. The sources of information relating to the specific field can be derived from academic research, analyst reports and historical and future trends analysis.

   For example, if you are determining whether it is viable to become a journalist as a career, it is necessary to research the history of the media, and how it originated from newspaper and then how it transitioned with TV and social media.

   By collecting the information that could directly influence the potential to make the change, this improves the comprehensive overview of the analysis in determining whether the commitment is worth pursuing.

2. Analyse Current Trends of the Environment. Utilising the sources of information gathered, you can establish your own perspective of the previous trends of the change and determine whether the field is affected by potential technologies.

   The rise of the internet and its integration with software services combined with the use of data to establish AI is seen to impact many fields. Through being informed of the previous and current trends of your field of interest, you can establish whether the transition is likely to be impacted by technology.

   The effects of new technologies as from the first industrialisation will not be as direct as they are now where the increased production of goods can be simply analysed. If your field is affected by technology, comprehensively research the trends to the degree it will potentially impact you within the future.

   As a result, you can be informed of the changes prior to outlining whether the change is viable to undertake.

3. Outline the Benefits, Drawbacks, Risks and Opportunities. Acknowledging your strengths and weaknesses provides a comprehensive outline in determining the benefits, drawbacks, risks and opportunities of the change.

   It is also necessary to include your existing commitments that you are required to carry out during the process of the change. This will provide

an overview of the internal traits as well as the external factors that establish whether the change is viable.
4. Make a Case for and against the Change. Now that you have made a comprehensive overview of the viability of the change, make a case to determine whether the change is worthwhile to carry out.

   This involves using the feasibility overview in 3, while also considering your present and future sentiments—regret, anticipation, doubt, dissatisfaction and fulfilment.
5. From this case, you are then able to make an informed evaluation in determining whether the change is worthwhile to undertake.

The Informed Change Analysis requires the awareness of yourself, the circumstance, and the context of your environment to make an informed decision. It is through the evaluation of these variables that you will justify undertaking the change or non-change.

Being aware of the advantages and disadvantages brings greater certainty in your decision which reduces your uncertainties. Having attained self-awareness along with undertaking an informed change analysis will lead to making decisions that is aligned towards personally desired outcomes.

The impartial stance in being receptive to change minimises a person's risk to experience setbacks and improves the ability to experience growth. To obtain progress involves changing when it is only viable to change.

Being flexible and willing to change eliminates any psychological anchors that restrict one's open-mindedness toward new possibilities. As a result, remaining open-minded leads to the potential of improving a person's current circumstances.

There are individuals who want to carry out the same routines on a consistent basis. This may be the effect of remaining comfortable with their current circumstance, or alternatively they may want to disregard the thought of any risk.

While this approach is temporarily viable, it is not risk averse in the twenty-first century where the world is changing correlative to that of the first industrialisation. It is necessary to evaluate the need to change in order to minimise setbacks, even if the pursued fields of people's interests are not directly affected by technological advancements.

Making an informed decision allows you to also predict future changes which ensures that a person does not hinder their own future potential.

To undertake viable changes requires you to proceed forward. Using the four steps to make the informed change analysis, its probe can be used as to determine whether change is worthwhile to make. By determining the present and future costs of the viability of change from the informed change analysis, people are able to:

1. Bring clarity to align people's beliefs, thoughts and actions.
2. Evaluate the actions that best adhere to one's values and objectives.
3. Carry out the actions that result in positively weighed outcomes.
4. Establish the ability to refine the implementation of change.
5. Improve their ability to capitalise on any future changes.

The initial phases of change often present obstacles. This is where being focused towards the benefits of the change will keep you motivated throughout the process of transition.

During the period of change, people will experience the sentiments of discouragement, curiosity and motivation depending on each phase. As people undertake changes that are advantageous, the habit of change is established. It is then how people decide to respond to change that leads to the gain of optimal results.

> Motivation is what gets you started. Habit is what keeps you going.
> —Jim Ryun

Habits Of Change

Humans constantly develop habits for the brain to save effort in thinking. The process of carrying out change also ensues in a habit of consecutive transitions. The initial act upon change is a decision carried out with courage and the subsequent actions involve experimentation.

These are followed with using your procedural memory to repeat the initial action or behaviour. After a series of carrying out these changes, this routine begins to form a habit.

Research conducted by psychologist Phillipa Laly, et al., states that a habit can be formed from the behaviours of exercising, eating and drinking after eighteen days at the earliest, with the average time requiring sixty-six days, and 254 days at the longest.

After a habit has been formed, the brain becomes less active as the cognition that was required to process information is replaced with the memory structure. The mind then simply recalls the prior actions after the change has been successfully carried out.

The initial phase of change will often experience a mismatch between perspective and reality. This will ensue with the forming of displeasure that hinders the process of carrying out the transition.

The reasons for approving the change include recognising its benefits and then reinforcing the propensity toward action and overcoming the setbacks. Through experimentations of the viable processes, this subsequently leads to the integration of change. These cycles of change are shown in Figure 9.

Figure 9–The Stages of the Change Curve

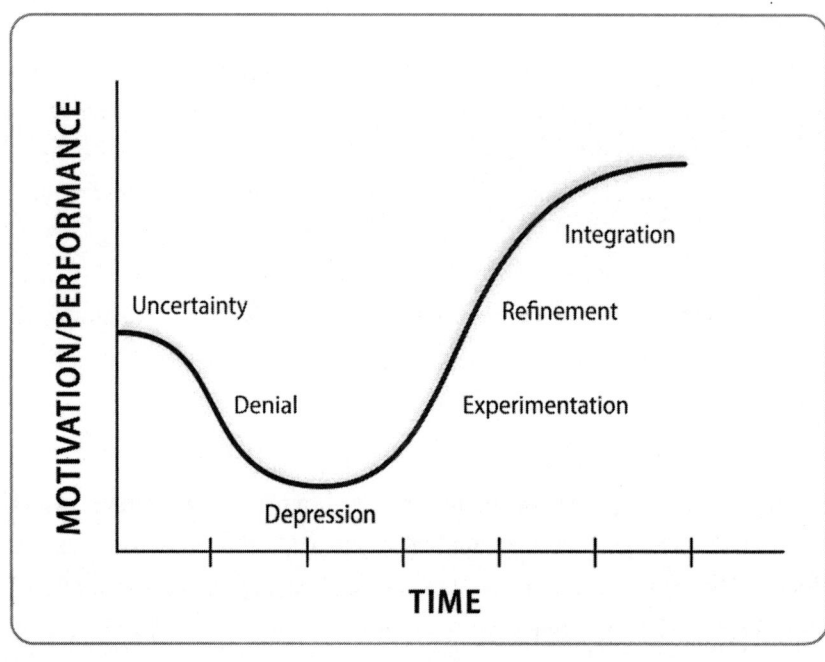

Many of the emotive mechanisms including denial, frustration and regret are direct impulses from the unconscious mind. Humans are psychologically hardwired to gain the most amount of reward from the least amount of effort.

This is the reason why the mind unconsciously prefers to pursue the prior routine and resists actions for change and growth. These unconscious mechanisms act as psychological drawbacks and when consciously recognised, must be disregarded in the process of change.

People who are willing to attain the future benefits of change, form the perseverance to obtain growth. It is through overcoming difficulties during the denial and displeasure phases of the transition that individuals are able to receive the rewards.

After the experimentation phase, the viable routine undergoes refinements and integrates into a set routine. This process of change can form into a habit and the propensity to grow.

The Progressive Mindset

The twenty-first century is the result of continual improvements made throughout the span of human existence. A greater accessibility of information has increased the ability for humans to attain knowledge and experience growth.

However, as the process of change can lead to long periods of setbacks without receiving any results, experiencing this adversity demotivates individuals. The progressive mindset focuses on embracing challenges as part of the process in order to attain long-term growth.

This involves shifting the conventional reward system within the process of the transition rather than being fixated on achieving the end result.

Adversity is often perceived as the impediment to growth. However, it is also through overcoming the challenges that people can refine their self-discipline. The renowned psychologist Abraham Maslow states that if people achieve less than what they are capable of, then they are likely to regret it in hindsight.

By shifting your perception from the impediments of hardships to the opportunities for growth, the progressive mindset establishes the motivation to focus on the process in order to complete the change.

This involves rewarding yourself with positive sentiments while facing challenges that manifest the experience of progress prior to the accomplishment of the result.

By establishing a reward system of motivation during the process of change, you are then able to focus on the process before the attainment of the result.

It is through this change in the perception of your focus that experiencing the obstacles can be viewed positively in order to obtain growth. In summary, the progressive mindset allows people to focus on the processes that lead to attainment of the result.

Progress is the result of undertaking changes based on the evaluation that the present is an improvement of the past. Since the integration of new routines is required to be developed from experimentation, it is beneficial to progress in increments that adhere to your level of comfort so that you can achieve your goals.

This means that to consistently progress requires you to adhere to your own sentiments and needs. For example, Jessica would like to begin undertaking meditation as a means to practice her mindfulness, and her goal is to be able to meditate for twenty minutes during each session.

However, due to restlessness, she has only been able to initially achieve ten minutes of meditation. For this circumstance, it is necessary to become accustomed to the ten-minute routine of meditation and she begins by increasing her time in increments at a level that is not overbearing.

This will guide her to feel temporary achievements. It is through recognising that the twenty-minute meditation goal is a process that will be achieved through the practice of consistency that leads to focusing within the present.

After people use their routine as an existing platform, they can then increase the propensity to change at a level that satisfies their willingness to remain motivated. Through forming a routine to then refine the prior actions, people are then able to refine the ability to progress over the long term.

Adopting a progressive mindset is where the individual is continually focused on carrying out positive changes despite the experience of any setbacks. Since the process of change includes a phase of experimentation, it is anticipated that setbacks will initially occur.

Therefore, by setting the expectation toward experiencing short-term setbacks, people are then prepared to overcome the initial difficulties.

The progressive mindset does not require every phase of change to achieve positive results, but rather focuses on the need to advance with a willingness to grow over time. During the process of change, individuals may decide to force themselves to make substantial progress as a result of setting high expectations.

However, it is due to setting such expectations that individuals will feel frustrated and discontent when there is deviation from the expectation. As a result, this will cause predicaments within one's beliefs to overcome the difficulties in order to change.

The central aim of the progressive mindset is to utilise and attain additional knowledge such that people can obtain their optimal results. Acquired through the mediums of experience and education, the premise of knowledge is to further a person's understanding of themselves and the world.

It is through the attainment of knowledge that leads to new perceptions, beliefs, actions and habits. As a result, through this process, individuals are able to apply the knowledge that then becomes part of their skills.

There are two different approaches that can be combined to accelerate people's progressive capabilities. Proposed by social anthropologist, John Lave, and educational practitioner, Étienne Wenger, the situated learning approach focuses on acquiring skills and knowledge through the application in its environment.

By actively participating in its intended context, individuals will immerse themselves in creating their own purpose from their experiences. This includes the acts of:

1. Cooperative education where the learned information is applied from a theory-to-work environment. This can include studying for a degree or course while applying the learned contents in an internship program.
2. Practicing the task and replicating the events, such as physical education in its intended real-life environment, i.e., at a sporting facility.
3. Replicating the environmental setting using work simulations or demonstration programs, i.e., using manoeuvre, hauling, driving and flight simulations.
4. Using the research content followed by applying it in its context.

The situated learning process utilises constructs of the individual's knowledge in forming their own skills that is practiced in the environment. By applying the knowledge in the appropriate environment, this forms the ability to attain skills through the application of their experience.

In contrast to the situated learning style, traditional learning focuses on planned learning processes that take place in educational institutions. Information is obtained through the teaching of theories, processes, structures and models in order to be assimilated into knowledge.

The formal teaching method presents task-governing conditions that enable individuals to prepare for the real-life application.

Correspondingly, the traditional learning method provides the adequate fundamental theory to prepare individuals to understand all viable aspects of the real-life application. People will then benefit from using the traditional learning method before applying the situated learning approach.

This is because with a greater theoretical understanding of the fundamental background knowledge, people are able to be more informed when applying it to skills.

Therefore, both learning strategies complement one another. Without fundamental background knowledge, situated learning methods would be ineffective when faced with out-of-context circumstances.

Conversely, traditional learning is challenging to assimilate without its real-life application. By applying the traditional and situated knowledge to its real-life application, this guides individuals to effectively obtain progress.

Now many individuals initially adopt a progressive mindset and apply both the situated and traditional learning approaches. However, individuals who become comfortable with their established routine will often decide to reduce their willingness to change.

This tendency will form into a fixed mindset and is not optimal to responding to the changes made in modern society. This is evident in many occupations, such as finance, marketing and project management where new software and technologies lead to new processes in order to facilitate the ability to produce work. With a progressive mindset, people can remain updated and position themselves to benefit from future changes.

The difference between a fixed and a progressive mindset is minor, however, the effects are significant. If a person adopts a progressive mindset rather than a fixed mindset in the context of learning the same amount of information, the person would absorb the information in a manner that allows them to recall and reapply the knowledge.

On the other hand, if the person adopted a fixed mindset, they would view what has already been learned as a means to become competent. This indicates that when assimilating new skills, a person who has adopted a progressive mindset will be able to apply greater amounts of knowledge to further their ability to form new competencies.

The result from adopting a progressive mindset rather than a fixed mindset is the disparity of the ability to obtain knowledge. Figure 10 shows that a person with a progressive mindset will expand their circle of knowledge which leads to the improvement of their skills.

Conversely, a fixed mindset will ensue when a person creates a mental boundary that prevents them from expanding their circle of knowledge.

Unfortunately, experiencing any future growth that the individual will obtain is limited by their fixed mindset.

Figure 10–Circle of Knowledge and Importance

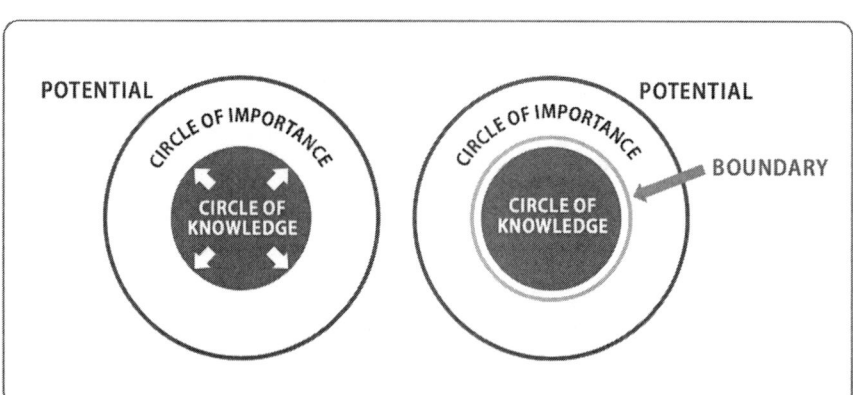

With a progressive mindset and by setting the right goals from the optimal goal setting, it will enable people to focus productively in a manner that minimises their uncertainties.

Over time, the person will accumulate more knowledge that will transfer into refining their skills and abilities. This will make the person more inclined to not only face adversities, but also will become more accustomed to experiencing temporary setbacks. With such objectives becoming increasingly fulfilled, the person will then be able to reach their potential.

The results of the progressive mindset are exemplified by the achievements of Ludwig van Beethoven.

The Progressive Mindset of Ludwig Van Beethoven

Ludwig van Beethoven devoted a predominant part of his life to composing music. At the age of twenty-one, Ludwig moved to Vienna where he began studying composition and slowly established a reputation for his work.

He embarked on his first tour at the age of twenty-seven but he was subject to early symptoms of hearing impairment. Throughout the next two decades, he continued composing his music with a progressive deterioration of his hearing.

He attempted to use different forms of hearing aids, including the apparatus of ear trumpets and bone-conduction techniques in order to listen to music. By the age of thirty-eight, Ludwig's hearing worsened and he had to rely on using written forms of communication among people through conversation books.

Many of his later compositions were produced when he was almost completely deaf, which included the last five string quartets, the *Missa Solemnis* and *Für Elise*.

Researchers from Amsterdam's Swammerdam Institute for Life Sciences were able to show Beethoven's three changes in composition style as his hearing condition worsened.

Earlier in his life, his compositions included high notes, but as his hearing started to become problematic, he began to use middle and low frequency notes more often. The composition of these lower-pitched notes allowed him to hear better when he composed his music.

When he was almost deaf, being only able to hear with his inner ear, he became compelled to use his imagination to produce music. He returned to his earlier composing style of using higher frequency notes.

It was through pivoting from his hearing adversity that led to reaching his potential as he returned to his natural musical element. Beethoven produced some of his most admired works including the *String Quartet No. 14* and the *Ninth Symphony* during his later years.

Understand that despite the adversities Beethoven faced, his own need to progress established the perseverance required to overcome his hardships. It was Beethoven's own mindset that allowed him to overcome his hearing difficulty and continue his music aspirations.

As a result, despite being deaf, Beethoven consistently composed musical pieces of art that encompassed the spirit of humanism.

Beethoven remained devoted to pursuing his musical objectives as he was required to change his musical style several times; this formed his perseverance during his hardships of hearing. He continued to practice and sought remedies for continuing his perfection in the art of sounds.

As his circle of knowledge required him to find remedies for his hearing loss, Beethoven utilised different methods of hearing aids. This allowed him to increase his circle of knowledge and circle of importance, which subsequently furthered his ability to produce new musical works.

Using decades of his musical experience along with preparing for his hearing deafness, Beethoven manifested the musical notes of instruments in his memory. Despite being almost deaf by the age of thirty-eight, Beethoven would remain composing music throughout his later years.

It was through Beethoven's progressive mindset that upheld his willingness to overcome the hardships which resulted in the achievement of his musical goals.

> Don't only practice your art, but force your way into its secrets, for it and knowledge can raise men to the divine.
> —Beethoven

The Twenty-First Century Environment

Humans have continued to progress throughout the course of history by utilising technologies to help fulfil people's needs and desires. The twenty-first century has seen an increase in the digital, software and artificial environments. Information technology has undergone major developments from the conventional use of the internet that has transitioned from the spreading of information toward improving connectivity of the globalised world.

This has resulted in consumers benefiting from changes in the production of goods and the provision of services. As a result, jobs that had no perceived value were made redundant and were replaced with roles in emerging sectors.

In the twenty-first century, there are new technologies including the Internet of Things, Artificial Intelligence (AI) and autonomous vehicles that will shape the future developments made in society.

The increasing connectedness of the globalised world has seen the transition of integrating technologies together that have facilitated new roles and opportunities in commerce. These technological improvements will transfer over into the agricultural, finance, biotechnology, construction and environmental sustainability sectors.

It is in the advancements made in technology that have resulted in social implications including the change in people's needs and interests which impact the opportunities presented in society.

In the whole, people have been able to benefit from the advancements made in technology that have resulted in the improvements made in their quality of lives. However, it is from prioritising people's ability to be able to fulfil their standards of living which impacts them on a considerable level.

It is, therefore, necessary from the individual level that people analyse whether the technological changes affect the fields of their career and objectives.

While IT has changed since the previous century, this sector remains as one of the primary drivers responsible for the improvement of knowledge attainment among people throughout the world. The internet has also provided the medium to connected users of sharing information through videos, texts and images.

We are now able to gain an unprecedented access to information of all topics and content. The increasing amount of material available is in theory supposed to enable people to become more knowledgeable. Within the formal educational field, this is apparent as the content is filtered appropriately and the information remains credible.

However, the accumulation of unfiltered information along with a lack of credibility in unverified sources reveals ambiguity and conflicting arguments, which makes it difficult to self-learn and attain knowledge. This has resulted in the challenge for people to filter and attain knowledge within the personal setting.

It is through such personal endeavours that allow people to recognise which aspirations they would like to experiment and pursue.

To effectively attain knowledge, it is important to understand how the mind filters and stores information. Research from Harvard psychologist George Miller has revealed that adults can store on average seven pieces of information in their short-term memory (lasting up to thirty seconds).

If the short-term memory is full from the accumulation of information, the new information pushes out part of the old information. For the mind to store any form of content, people are required to consolidate the information from the short-term working memory into the long-term memory.

It is, therefore, important to address the conflicting content in the short term in order to make the allocation space for storing knowledge so that it can be transferred into long-term memory.

If there are differences within the perspective in a topic, this leads to an accumulation of unnecessary information that reduces the storage capacity and ability to store knowledge.

While it has been more challenging in the twenty-first century for people to attain their own expertise in the modern fields, recognising how the mind filters information leads to the opportunity for people to refine their knowledge in their career fields and interests.

Technological developments made via the internet have led to the emergence of new roles and opportunities. During the 1990s, many people were reluctant to embrace the benefits of the internet due to the neglect and avoidance of change.

While many sectors including the decline of traditional retail were negatively affected by the emergence of online businesses, new jobs have also been created. This includes global sourcing, programmers, data analytics and graphic designers.

Job roles have also shifted in the retail environment as project management, warehousing and customer service have seen new opportunities that have replaced the number of sales clerks in order to compete with the online shopping environment.

The development of new career fields is reflected in the field of marketing, where digital online services are becoming an increasingly used method to advertise compared to traditional marketing.

While the improvements made in technological advancements have made certain roles redundant, new jobs have also been created within the same sector. The internet has also improved options for customers by enabling online purchases and faster delivery of products.

As a result, this has led to increased competition throughout the business and consumer sectors.

Globalisation has developed over the last two decades, which has led to the interconnectedness among countries. This has resulted in the increase in acceptance and the embracing of different cultures all around the world.

As relationships between nations have improved, the transfer of technology has assisted humans in performing laborious tasks and this has enabled many citizens to gain a better quality of life. The International Monetary Fund (IMF) states that technological advancements are a key driver responsible for the improvement of income and living standards.

Since trade and commerce currently takes place on a global scale, this has resulted in a more effective use of resources and skilled employment. Individuals can benefit from trends of the globalised world by specialising in their career or aspirations most appropriate within developed or developing regions.

With the trend of making continual progress in the globalised world, new opportunities are presented for individuals who are informed and are seeking to experience growth.

Similar to circumstance of the first industrialisation where individuals transitioned from a farming-based nation to a manufacturing- and industry-based economy, individuals who were willing to change reaped the benefits, while those who were unwilling to change experienced setbacks or became stagnant.

For the twenty-first century, a global supply chain exists whereby developed nations can concentrate on the development of new technologies, scientific research and higher quality goods and services. This is evident as the developed Group of Five Nations (G5) accounted for three-quarters of all the patents during the period from 1995 to 2014.

Developing countries on the other hand have opportunities to focus on the improvement of local infrastructure, education and the manufacturing of goods. With new opportunities available and the workforce being malleable, individuals can transition into career roles that are in-line with their strengths and interests in the regions that require that particular proficiency.

The globalised world has enabled the spread of technology, which has improved not only income, but also created new job roles that were previously non-existent in addition to reducing poverty.

The trend of technological advancements stipulated by the interconnectedness of the globalised world has resulted in many positive outcomes where individuals can benefit from technological and global opportunities.

As in any case of change, there are also apparent setbacks in the fields which have been perceived as inefficient and have been subsequently made redundant. This has included manufacturing in developed nations and traditional production methods in developing countries.

Individuals negatively affected by the changes are able to recognise the current environmental context such that they are able to prepare for opportunities made from the emerging technologies.

The new technologies currently emerging include innovations such as the Internet of Things, artificial intelligence (AI) and autonomous vehicles. The Internet of Things refers to the ability for technological devices to connect and operate over the internet without being in physical contact of the appliance.

In the household setting, lighting, media, entertainment systems, climate control and appliances can be operated remotely via the Internet of Things' network. This can enable people's personal criteria of household appliances to be set-in-specification and operate independently in an effective manner.

In the field of medical science, the monitoring of heart rate, blood pressure and advanced hearing aids inform users of their health condition over the system's network in near-real time. The Internet of Things is also used in manufacturing where data is collected to monitor the performance of machineries, which helps identify operational issues.

In addition to this, barcodes are also placed in the inputs and outputs of production which assist the management of the logistical network. These services have been made viable by the improvement of software combined with the seamless connectivity of the internet.

AI is increasingly used in the modern setting and refers to the use of digital computers and machine-controlled robots that solve problems and perform tasks without human intervention. Similar to the human mind, computers can store, retrieve and transmit data through the use of computer coding language.

AI is categorised in the form of strong and narrow AI, where the former is used to describe the ability of a machine to develop intellectual abilities similar to that of the human mind.

Currently, computer scientists are faced with many challenges in the development of strong AI due to the intricacies in emulating the neurophysiology and psychology of the human brain.

The majority of AI that is presently active is part of narrow AI, which refers to the learning capabilities of machines that have been programmed to complete a specific task.

One component of the narrow AI includes the expert system that assists humans in making decisions by using algorithms of code to interpret, plan and predict future data for making decisions.

This is used in medical check-ups and virus analysis, financial loan analysis, warehouse optimisation, transportation cargo scheduling, monitoring, controlling, planning and scheduling.

As a result, new jobs including computer scientists, data analysts, warehouse AI and machine servicing technicians are required to facilitate the expected growth within these fields.

Both narrow and strong AI are increasingly being used in the world to better process large datasets so industries can make informed decisions for future projects intended for commercial, government and social applications.

It is in people's individual and collective responsibility to be aware of the benefits and drawbacks AI brings to the whole, which will mitigate the unrighteous use of its applications.

New jobs including technological analysts, software engineers, AI and machine learning specialists, robotics applicator, digital and innovation transformation experts and interactive designers are required in the narrow and strong AI fields.

Driverless cars have also been using AI within the feature applications, which are predicted to be available in the near future. Operating autonomously requires a combination of sensors, including road infrastructure and car-inbuilt sensors.

This includes GPS, light detection and ranging, odometry, radar and inertial measuring units. Many of these sensors incorporate narrow AI components including expert system and machine learning.

There are currently six levels of autonomy published by the Society of Automotive Engineers (SAE) and their guideline of classification levels include: 0. No automation, 1. Driver assistance, 2. Partial automation, 3. Conditional automation, 4. High automation, 5. Complete automation.

Most modern vehicles qualify for level one whereby the driver will be guided by slight technological aid such as adaptive cruise control and lane-keeping assistance.

Car manufacturers including General Motors, Tesla, Mercedes-Benz and Nissan have been able to produce cars with partial automation capabilities whereby the automated system takes control of the acceleration, braking and steering with the driver required to remain alert to take control of the vehicle when necessary.

There has been ongoing research, development and testing undertaken by car manufacturing that strives to improve the ability of machines to replace the need for human driving and awareness.

This is where car companies now require an increasing number of perception software engineers, logistical dispatchers, teleoperations and function safety technicians.

With the developments of emerging technologies including the Internet of Things, AI processes and autonomous cars, the technological landscape is anticipated to advance further just as the first industrial revolution paved the way for the growth towards traditional manufacturing.

Many of these emerging technologies will later be able to be transferred to other sectors that prove beneficial to servicing people's needs. This includes healthcare, human relations, customer service, marketing, home maintenance and other traditional service sector roles.

By being informed of the direction in where technology is headed, you can direct your progress toward obtaining your desired future objective. If your field of interest is affected or indirectly affected by these fields, you can carry out an informed change analysis to determine whether it is beneficial to change.

This will minimise the risks from any future changes such that you are able to achieve your career and personal objectives with self-fulfilment.

Key Points

1. The first industrial revolution experienced major changes as citizens were required to respond to transitions by shifting their occupations and objectives.
2. Opportunities and redundancies were made during the first industrialisation as a majority of the population that had been working in the agricultural industry were required to find new work in cities that offered higher wages.
3. The middle class emerged during the industrial revolution as the production of goods and provision of services increased during this period.
4. The Informed Change Analysis evaluates the personal traits and the external commitments using the four steps to determine the viability of change.
5. It is not always advantageous to change, however, it is important to be receptive to new circumstances.
6. Being informed from the case of change allows people to minimise setbacks while also being able to benefit from worthwhile opportunities.
7. The progressive mindset focuses on attaining consistent growth by pursuing goals with the setting of optimal expectations. By using internal motivation, the reward system is shifted toward the process required to complete objectives.
8. To enhance the propensity toward growth involves attaining knowledge from combining the situated and traditional learning approaches.

9. The circle of knowledge increases through acquiring new skills that lead to furthering the completion of the circle of importance.
10. As the objectives have been increasingly fulfilled within the circle of importance, this leads to the pursuit of new objectives that further an individual's potential.
11. Ludwig van Beethoven consistently composed music despite being almost completely deaf during middle age. During his later years, Beethoven produced some of his most admired works.
12. The twenty-first century has experienced major changes including an increased worldwide connectivity of the internet that has furthered the expansion of globalisation.
13. The Internet of Things, AI and autonomous vehicles are technologies that will soon emerge within the future of society.
14. Such new technological advances will transfer into the finance, marketing, biotechnology, construction, agriculture and environmental sustainability sectors.
15. There are new opportunities in the twenty-first century in which people are able to benefit by accomplishing their objectives with self-fulfilment.
16. It is then up to people's willingness and inner confidence that inspires their forward action.

Chapter 5
Inspire Yourself or Who Will?

The human potential is often measured by the means of natural brilliance, favourable circumstances and hard work. What is often left unnoticed is the importance of self-belief, which either facilitates or impedes a person's progress toward meeting their potential.

What a person is capable of achieving cannot be realised until they have the confidence to reinforce their actions. By developing consistent levels of confidence cultivated from self-belief, you are able to direct your energies to fulfilling your objectives.

As a result, you will begin to reduce your doubts from uncertainties, improve your relationships and enhance your self-worth. This result of utilising one's own self-confidence is represented by the Wright brothers who were able to find the solution of the first flight without any previous aeronautical experience.

The Story of The Wright Brothers

Wilbur and Orville Wright were brothers born four years apart and they both shared a fondness for pursuing creative interests that aroused their curiosities. While it was recognised in the family that education was a main priority, neither of the brothers formally graduated high school.

Wilbur Wright, the older of the two brothers, originally intended to attend college but became seriously injured in the face when another player hit him with a hockey stick during an ice hockey game in the winter of 1885–86. With his original aspirations crushed, he spent the next three years at home caring for his terminally ill mother who suffered from tuberculosis.

During this period, Wilbur also experienced depression and read books from his father's library during his spare time. Following their mother's death, Orville spent several summers learning the printing trade and persuaded Wilbur to start their own printing business.

In 1889, the brothers entered the printing industry by providing professional printing services and they also launched their own newspaper called *The West Side News*. Orville was responsible for publishing the paper while Wilbur served as the newspaper's editor.

Their printing business faced fierce competition from established newspaper companies. After a year of newspaper publications, the Wrights were unable to compete and decided to focus their attention on printing services before later selling the business.

The bicycle craze began and the brothers decided to pursue their interests in this sector. Wilbur and Orville opened a bicycle shop in 1892, which fixed, rented and sold bikes. In Dayton, Ohio, where they opened the shop, the town had only twelve miles of paved streets, which caused dust to settle in the wheel bearings and that resulted in excessive wear to the bikes.

Naturally inclined to strive and make improvements, the Wright brothers decided to address this issue by designing their own bicycles in 1895. Four years after the bicycle business started, they introduced the "Van Cleve," which was a handmade bicycle with a variety of choices in handlebars, including metal or wooden rims and single or double-tube pneumatic tires.

Throughout the years of designing and manufacturing bicycles, Wilbur and Orville's future bicycles included sealed wheel bearings with felt washers and a self-lubricating oil hub. This reduced the maintenance and wear from riding, a feature that is still used in modern bicycles.

The Wright brothers also designed their own version of their coaster brake which provided additional riding support in their bicycles. The Wright brothers had the interest to constantly strive toward improving the designs of their bicycles. This allowed them to be at the forefront of cycling technology that later proved beneficial in their aeronautical pursuits.

While working in the bicycle shop, the brothers read a report of a flying incident that led to Otto Lilienthal's death in 1896. This German glider pioneer was responsible for building a glider capable of gliding over 800 feet or 240 meters and this was achieved by making improvements in the wing components.

During the same year as Otto Lilienthal's passing, scientist Samuel Langley from the Smithsonian Institution began flying a steam-powered model aircraft, but the flights remained problematic.

It was during this period that the Wright brothers recognised an opportunity and developed an interest in flying. Wilbur and Orville spent the next few years researching aerodynamics.

Having exhausted the resources from the local library, Wilbur wrote a letter to Samuel Langley at the Smithsonian Institution requesting information and publications of aeronautical designs. Utilising the knowledge gathered from Otto Lilienthal, Samuel Langley, Leonardo da Vinci and others, the Wright brothers began their mechanical aeronautical experimentation in 1899.

Studying the problems encountered by previous flyers, the Wright brothers sought professional opinions and corresponded with Octave Chanute, an aeronautic pioneer who had flown an aircraft based on the braced multiplane design.

Octave, originally a self-taught civil engineer, applied the trussing system that was used in the bridge architectural designs to calculate the strength required to sustain the weight of the aircraft's structure.

The glider that Octave Chanute designed was known as the most stable and sophisticated at the time. This provided the Wright brothers with a foundation and a starting point for their structural designs.

The Wright brothers also sought to find fundamental answers to the problem of flight through observing large gliding birds. Wilbur saw that the birds kept lateral balance by the lateral curving movements of their wingtips.

Later, the brothers came up with the design of an aircraft with the capability of adjusting the angle direction of the wings, which was a technique that became known as wing warping. It was through recognising the fundamental issues of flight and from studying previous aeronautical professionals that the Wright brothers concluded that maintaining control of the aircraft while in flight would be the most important aspect when flying long distances.

The Wright brothers began testing unpowered aircrafts from 1899 to 1902 with the goal of refining their ideas of flight. The first aircrafts flown were an unpiloted kite followed by gliders with the purpose of testing their ideas of aerodynamic performance and flight control.

All these tests took place in Kitty Hawk, North Carolina, which was a favoured location due to the consistent high winds. These experiments enabled Wilbur and Orville to understand that a free flying object had to be controlled in a similar manner to cycling.

For a rider to maintain control of their bicycle, they were dependent upon the steering and pedalling functions. The Wright brothers proposed that to stay in flight, the pilot needed to control the rotational motion of an airplane. In flight, the aircraft rotated around three rotational axes named roll, pitch and yaw.

Figure 11–Axes of an Airplane

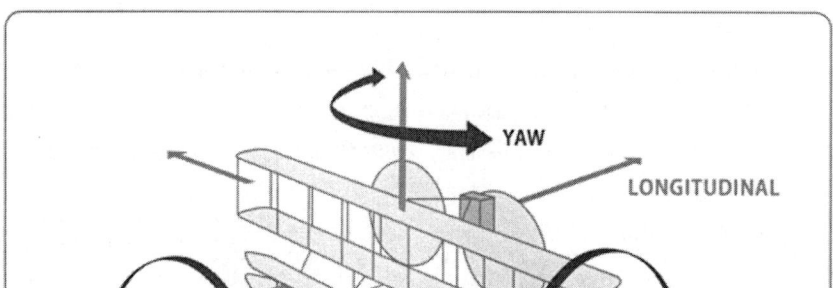

After developing the rotational framework in aerodynamics, the brothers also proposed the need to control the aircraft in all directions. They experimented with the gliders to determine whether such a hypothesis would hold true.

The first glider design did not produce enough lift and this was subsequently followed with another design that lacked in aerodynamic manoeuvre and control.

Wilbur and Orville then collected data for analysing the effects of wind tunnels and how it would affect a glider's lift and drag. This led to making design refinements for the wings for future gliders. The third glider constructed in 1902 generated sufficient lift to make long glides.

In this design, the usual feature of a wing and elevator was incorporated, but it also included a newly designed rear rudder that was responsible for controlling the yaw axis. For the first time, an aircraft could be entirely controlled by a pilot in all three aerodynamic axes.

After making this progress, Wilbur and Orville believed they were ready to begin designing an engine for the airplane.

With the major aerodynamic problems of manoeuvre and control now addressed, the brothers were then required to construct an engine appropriate for propelling and maintaining a controlled flight. It was decided by the Wrights that the engine needed to produce at least eight horsepower and weigh not more than 200 pounds or eighty-one kilograms.

Realising that the automotive market had no available designs that fit these criteria, Wilbur and Orville planned to build their own. A nearby brass works acquaintance advised them that the engine would save weight if they would cast the engine using aluminium.

They settled on a four-cylinder design, similar to that of car engines built during the same period. The brothers built the engine block while rehiring a local machinist, Charles Taylor, from their bicycle business in order to produce and assemble the parts.

The final step was to include propellers in the aircraft to generate the thrust using the power produced from the engine. Scientist Samuel Langley from the Smithsonian Institution had previously reported from his research that there is a significant relation between maritime and aerial propellers.

The Wright brothers conducted experiments and collected empirical (based from observation or experience) data to determine the difference between water to air pressure and to estimate the power that the propellers needed to produce flight.

Similar to solving their issues on aerodynamics and maintaining control in aviation, Wilbur and Orville determined the propeller design by first conceptualising the issue by mentally developing a testable theory. Often the brothers brainstormed their ideas and strenuously debated prior to deciding on a viable solution.

Rather than constructing a solution based on the results from an aerial propulsion experiment, the brothers proposed to approach the propeller features separate from the winged surface with the intention of producing lift from thrust.

After three months of effort, the twin propeller design was developed and two propellers were positioned behind both wings to power the aircraft from behind. Through solving the problems in the field of aerodynamics by coming up with independent solutions to produce lift, manoeuvre, control and power the aircraft, the Wright brothers were able to complete their first successful flight.

After seven years of attempting to unravel the solution for human flight, the Wright brothers piloted Flyer I on 17 December 1903, to more than twenty feet, covering a distance of 37 meters or 120 feet.

This event marked the beginning of the pioneer era of modern aviation. Consequently, the possibility of travelling through the mobility of flight then experienced significant improvements in the future.

What is important here is the self-belief of Wilbur and Orville Wright. Without any aeronautical background, the brothers managed to create a solution to sustain control for the first flight. There were competitors within this aviation pursuit that had more appropriate credentials, better financial backing and aeronautical experience.

However, the Wright brothers had the self-belief to exercise discipline, dedication and perseverance which allowed them to develop their own unique approach to problem-solving. It is from this inner confidence of the Wright brothers that led to the research, testing and experimentation that resulted in the first controlled flight.

The Self-Belief of The Wright Brothers

The Wright brothers' journey began with an interest in flying but was completed as a result of their self-belief. Orville stated, "We were interested in flying as a sport" and this established the motivation for beginning their aeronautical pursuits.

It was from the brothers' interest in flight combined with their surrounding environment that encouraged them to pursue such objective. This is reflected in Orville's quote by stating that they grew up, "in an environment where there was always much encouragement to children to pursue intellectual interests; to investigate whatever aroused curiosity."

Their ventures into the printing, cycling and aviation industries repeatedly involved learning the fundamental components before gaining experience from the application of each field. The need to further their objectives then led to the brothers' own reliance to cultivate self-belief in finding the solution to problems.

As a result, they established a framework of problem-solving by using their knowledge to improvise and pursue their innovations. It was through their initial fascination of their interests that led to the honing of their self-belief that established the processes required to accomplish their objectives.

The Wright brothers undertook rigorous methods during the forming and testing of their theories. They carried out experiments to determine the accuracy of their various hypotheses.

Whether the results of their experiments were right or wrong held no significance, but rather, it was from accruing the knowledge from these results that held importance. This is because the findings of such experiments allowed the Wright brothers to direct their efforts onto the path of finding the solution.

In their pursuit toward solving the first flight, it was through this rigorous process that proved the difference between the Wright brothers and their competitors.

Many of the competitors had focused their efforts on how an aircraft would behave during flight when integrated with power while others concentrated on past flight innovations. The difference between the Wrights and their competitors was that through their own self-belief they were able to analyse and break down the problem of flight to lift, power and control. Wilbur and Orville were then able to systematically test and solve each of the problems to aerodynamics independently.

Without the inner confidence in their own capabilities, Wilbur and Orville not have effectively challenged the prior methods of aeronautical experiments and developed their own strategies to inaugurate the first sustained flight.

It was their self-belief of the Wright's that reinforced their diligence to research the aeronautical foundations and break down each issue so the solutions could be identified, hypothesised and experimented.

Wilbur and Orville would use their confidence to remain resilient from their failures by reinforcing that temporary setbacks are expected to be a part of the experimental process.

As such, it is through the Wright brothers' own intrinsic set of beliefs that directed their abilities to solve the solution of the first flight.

What is often disregarded in the process of carrying out any pursuit is that it requires a myriad of experimentation that results in multiple setbacks before a breakthrough. In the Wright brothers' case to innovate, they recognised that temporary failures were a part of the experimental process.

With their self-beliefs, they were focused on what had worked and they integrated the setbacks as experience to refine their hypotheses. This allowed them to efficiently establish their own methodology to innovate. From the seven years of repeated research and experimentation, the Wright brothers combined their solutions, which led to the accomplishment of the first sustained flight.

> If we worked on the assumption that what is accepted as true really is true, then there would be little hope for advance.
>
> —Orville Wright

The Value of Self-Belief

Self-belief is crucial in the twenty-first century society that places high value on confidence. People's skills and capabilities are perceived based on their self-belief, which in turn projects their confidence.

However, it is common for individuals to give others the impression of confidence without establishing an awareness of their own identity. This pseudo-derived form of self-belief limits the awareness of an individual's own understanding of their perceptions, beliefs and actions.

Self-belief is referred to as having attained clear self-awareness of your own abilities. On the other hand, confidence occurs when your thoughts, skills and abilities are in alignment with your character. The precursor to confidence is to have obtained self-belief.

People that have established self-belief, are then able to project their confidence that had formed from within. It is through understanding the awareness of your intrinsic self that allows you to reinforce your potential.

Self-belief is a psychological affirmation of the individual's capabilities that directs them to establish informed decisions. The study of behaviourism expanded with cognitive theories in the latter half of the twentieth century which highlighted the importance of recognising one's capabilities in relation to their commitments.

This is exemplified in the research carried out by retired professors Susan Harter of psychology and John Graham Nicholls of physiology who have revealed that the perception of people's own abilities is the central mediating construct toward their achievement. Through people's own self-awareness and by utilising their own skills and abilities, they can attain self-fulfilment.

Individuals that do not know their capabilities leads to confusion and misguidance in decisions which causes cognitive dissonance within their decision-making. It is through self-awareness that clarity is formed and aligns them with pursuing the commitments that coincide with their established values.

Accomplishing such objectives results in attaining a person's desired rewards. As a result, self-belief provides the ability for people to affirm certainty in their action.

Existing within the culture of the twenty-first century is the perception of confidence that has become associated with successful skills and abilities. This is not a surprise as it is in human nature that people strive to be widely accepted. Psychologically, the role of being confident is to reinforce a person's skills and abilities that influence people's decisions and actions.

Being confident without the foundation of self-awareness is establishing pseudo self-belief. This is where the spurious understanding of an individual's own self gives them the ability to act with confidence.

However, it is not beneficial for this individual to voice their views to others when they are uninformed. This will result in cognitive dissonance within their own beliefs and actions that will cause uncertainty in their future judgments and perceptions.

Through your own self-awareness, you can believe in your capabilities and feel confident in your decision-making. Confidence does not indicate that you are required to be accurate in your actions, but rather that you should have the *intention* to be correct.

It is from self-belief that leads to the development of consistent levels of confidence. As a result, you are able to reinforce your ability to express your own individuality throughout your everyday life.

Strategies to Develop Self-Belief

By establishing self-belief, you are able to phase out the doubts in your life that cause contradictory viewpoints in your perceptions. To develop self-belief that affirm your confidences involves the following process:

1. Reinforcing Your Foundations

All individuals encounter experiences where obstacles undermine the undertaking of their tasks. Recalling, and writing down your understanding of who you are by being aware of your thoughts, strengths, abilities and passions establishes the framework for developing your self-belief.

Through being aware of your character traits, you are able to reinforce your foundations that furthers your self-belief.

2. The Paradigm Shift of Knowledge

The knowledge attained from traditional and situated learning methods direct peoples to refine their decision-making abilities and will incentivise them to refine their skills. Improving one's knowledge reinforces their self-belief which gives them more competence.

Whether people obtain their knowledge through books, the internet, television or a formal education, the traditional learning method helps them refine their skills. The Wright brothers did not have any background or experience in aviation, but with determination toward their pursuit of flying, they invested time in researching, experimenting and reiterating their process to obtain aeronautical knowledge.

It was from the wide foundations of the Wright brothers' knowledge that they remained undeterred by setbacks until they accomplished their aeronautical goals. The knowledge attained from traditional and situated learning enhances people's ability to enhance their self-belief.

3. Assess and Replace Negative Thoughts

Negative thoughts come from unpleasant emotions that temporarily affect your sentiments in shaping your self-belief. The co-founder of Social Neuroscience, Professor John T Cacioppo, revealed from his research that a bias exists in the cognitive processing of information in the human mind that concentrates on negative thoughts rather than an equivalent positive.

This negative bias is connected to the fact that people's brains experience greater sensitivity toward unpleasant information. Establishing clarity in the way your mind behaves and reacts to information forms the ability to regulate your emotions and perceptions that influences your beliefs.

Minimising the natural tendency of having negative thoughts involves recognising when such perceptions initially occur. Subsequently, individuals that analyse the degree to which the negative thoughts affect their sentiments allows them to identify whether such thoughts are productive. By increasing your attention toward when the negative thoughts arrive, you are then able to promptly remove the sentiments from your frame of mind.

Psychological research recommends counteracting the negativity through conjuring repeated forms of positive reinforcements. This may include recalling and writing down positive statements or repeating positive affirmations in your mind.

Furthermore, a person is also able to practice mindfulness, which focuses on improving awareness of when unnecessary thoughts and emotions appear. By moderating one's thoughts from a negative-biased mind, this reinforces the development of forming self-belief.

4. Reinforce with Your Body Language

Your body language is an unspoken form of communication that uses physical behaviour to express your frame of mind. By shaping your own body posture according to psychologists, you can influence and regulate your subconscious emotional state.

The posture of pushing one's shoulders back displays self-belief. Conversely, when your back is hunched forward, it displays the signs of unease and defensiveness. Your facial expressions, arm and leg gestures and overall composure are other indications of your psychological frame of mind.

From remaining composed with a solid posture reinforces the self-belief on not only how you perceive yourself, but also on how other people perceive you.

Through revisiting your foundations and utilising your attained knowledge, you can establish your self-belief. Honing your thoughts and body language will reinforce your abilities. This will in turn form the coherence developed between your thoughts, skills and potential.

As a result, self-belief refines people's confidence to interact with others and the performing of the tasks that are in one's own alignment.

Cultivating Character

The model individual who has cultivated their own self-belief is one who is in control of their thoughts, beliefs and actions. Their opinions are expressed based on their competency as they respond to circumstances based from their knowledge on the topics of interest.

Rather than focusing on the experiences of their present objectives, the cultivated individual moderates their sentiment as a means of productively channelling their energies to accomplish their goals. It is this foundation of self-belief that leads to informed decisions and actions that reinforce their personal growth.

The cultivated individual aims to refine their circumstances of everyday life through being informed in the way they decide to interact in everyday activities.

This includes refining how they decide to make accurate decisions, goals and plans.

As previously outlined from the last section, our brains are hardwired with a psychological bias that is inclined towards finding problems and to observe for any danger. While we no longer face consistent threats to our physical survival as we might have since in previous centuries, we often expect the worst in situations.

This negative bias can cause unnecessary reactions to problems that do not have particularly dire consequences. For instance, you could believe that missing your flight will have terrible consequences and, therefore, you will initially worry, stress and overreact.

But in actuality, if you do miss your flight, you will just board the next one. The worst possible outcome that will happen is that you will be required to purchase another plane ticket.

Many of the problems people increasingly face in the twenty-first century are psychological issues. This includes problems associated with meeting the expectations we have set in terms of our daily tasks, circumstances and projection of our outward image.

People then form the desire to obtain and maintain such expectations that in turn shape their living standards. Due to the natural behaviour of the mind to sway toward a negative bias, this natural tendency has been proven to motivate the accomplishment of tasks meeting one's existing expectations.

This is evident from the research undertaken by Behavioural Scientist Kelly Goldsmith and Economist Ravi Dhar which has revealed that people are more motivated when there is an incentive to avoid losses than to experience a gain.

As a result, this indicates that people will stress toward meeting the expectation of preserving their existing gains. However, what a person had previously obtained may be not worthwhile to maintain. This is where it is necessary to recognise that the issues people anticipate may not be as significant as they had once initially perceived.

The cultivated individual recognises this negative inclination and has anticipated that the mind is expected to potentially exacerbate everyday issues. To address this behavioural tendency, it is optimal to frame the expectation of perceiving the problems primarily based off their degree of importance.

This can involve measuring whether the issue has protracted consequences that may affect one's circumstance over the short to long term. As a result, the cultivated person can form clarity in judgment by basing circumstances off their level of importance.

This will allow the model individual to recognise the issues that hold significance while disposing the matters that do not. Through this, the cultivated person can improve their ability to arrange and prioritise their obligations.

People that have established self-belief are able to use their confidence to complete the tasks by focusing on those that bear importance to them. By modelling the cultivated individual, you too are able to prioritise the fulfilling of obligations with optimal expectations.

A cultivated person utilises their confidence to reinforce their abilities toward achieving their objectives. This involves focusing on the performance of the quality of their decision-making, combined with their ability to accomplish their task.

This replaces the conventional approach where people develop motivation based off acquiring the result. By prioritising on the process that leads to the result, this refines the focus for individuals to achieve it.

This model of the cultivated character represents the ideal means for individuals to live once establishing self-belief and confidence. In the current world where many of our problems are psychological, increasing your understanding of the cognition of the mind allows you to regulate your thoughts with proficiency.

Through being informed of the negative bias, you are able to moderate your sentiments and prioritise objectives based on their degree of importance.

As a result, through refining your own self-belief and confidence, you too can cultivate your character that results in the ability to live optimally.

Key Points

1. The human potential is often disguised by the means of natural brilliance, favourable circumstances and hard work but disregards the value of self-belief and confidence.
2. Self-belief is referred to as having attained self-awareness of your own abilities.
3. The Wright brothers utilised their own self-belief to develop an efficient process for innovating in the fields of cycling and aeronautics.
4. Wilbur and Orville Wright developed a rigorous system of debate and discussion to come up with a series of hypotheses before testing out their ideas. The experiments that were viewed as failures held no significance as it was through their own belief systems that they acquired the solution of the first sustained flight.
5. The difference between the Wright brothers and their aviation competitors was that through their self-belief, they were able to achieve sustained flight by breaking down the fundamental issues into the solvable components of lift, aerodynamics and powering the aircraft.
6. To establish self-belief requires reinforcing your foundations and obtaining the paradigm shift from knowledge. To assess and replace negative thoughts while reinforcing your self-belief through your body language leads to the affirmation of your abilities.
7. The precursor of establishing confidence is to have obtained self-belief.
8. Confidence is developed when your perceptions, beliefs and skills are in alignment with your character.
9. The natural expression of a confident person associates with competency and being accepted within communicative and social settings.
10. A confident person does not require all actions to be accurate but rather to have the intention to be right.
11. The cultivated individual represents the ideal model for people to live effectively once having established their self-belief and confidence.
12. People are more motivated when there is an incentive to avoid losses than to experience a gain. What a person previously obtained may not be as significant as they had initially perceived.
13. It is through developing self-belief that people are able to enhance their perspective and navigate proficiently in the twenty-first century.

Chapter 6
The Enhanced Perspective

In modern society where the accumulation of information and opinions are widely accessible, the ideal perspective is often lost. From the confidence formed in your character, you are able to perceive situations in your life through enhanced frames of reference.

This involves evaluating the value of art and its importance in shaping the standards within the cultures of society. Through this, you are able to value genuine relationships and be informed of what is right in matters.

The Art of Purpose

The essence of art is expressed in the forms of music, literature, sculptures, paintings and cinematography. What is perceived to be 'good' art is subjective by the nature of its expression and how it is shaped from the circumstances of society.

People individually observe the external environment is in the same nature that coincides with shaping their own perspective of art. To assimilate the fundamental causes behind a person's own perspective, is to analyse the purpose of art. This will determine how master artists are able to create art beyond the dimension of its beauty.

A masterpiece in art is viewed with acclaim among the wider audience. Every work of art includes the expressive nature of the artist and yet only a few artists throughout the centuries have been able to consistently produce masterpieces.

The master artist combines their skill and effort to create an invitation of an emotive experience for their intended and wider audience. This is where such arts are able to showcase the emotions that represent elements within the culture of society.

As a result, the master artist is then able to shape and fulfil people's collective aspirations through their works of art.

To acquire the talent of the skilled artist requires the ability to portray an emotive experience that manifests within a person's perspective. Leo Tolstoy (9 September 1828 to 20 November 1910) is the author who wrote *War and Peace*, *Anna Karenina* and *The Death of Ivan Ilych*.

These three works of fiction present the intricacies of relationships and events that affect the lives of characters living within and away from the Russian aristocratic class. Tolstoy's learned talents exist from uncovering the psyche of his characters to emphasise to the reader how situations and choices have come about.

It is then, through the use of framing narratives that portray the outcome of the character's choices. This allows the reader to be immersed within the character's perspectives and they are able to reflect on the decision-making process as if it were their own.

Tolstoy presents the repercussions of the character's actions while exploring the concepts of love, loyalty, forgiveness, responsibility, family, relationships and individuality. Through his works, he articulates the intricacies of what it means to be human, so his readers can manifest their own understanding of their personal qualities.

In *War and Peace*, Prince Andrei Bolkonsky is subject to the dilemma of attempting to rekindle new love after his wife passes away. Andrei meets Natasha Rostova and they soon fall in love and become engaged before Andrei's father objects.

It was Andrei's father's opinion that he shouldn't rush into a marriage with a woman half his age and who was criticised for being in a lower social class. Natasha's parents requested that the wedding be delayed for a year.

This would potentially cause conflict between both families and caused resistance from one family, leading to difficulties for all parties.

Natasha tells her brother, Nikolai Rostov, that unlike her previous relationships, she feels, "at peace and settled. I know that no better man than he exists." However, the author presents Nikolai's introspection that questions why his sister is so insistent about this man despite the father's disapproval and the delay of marriage.

The reader learns that Nikolai "discovered, to his surprise" that it was because at the "depth of her soul [Natasha] too had many doubts about this marriage." The inclusion of internal monologues showcases the characters' internal beliefs and perceptions, which increase the depth of the characters' aptitude.

The author is able to concentrate on exploring the intricacies surrounding the motivations behind human behaviour, which gives readers the opportunity to contemplate viable courses of action.

As a result, the path undertaken by the characters provides an opportunity for the reader to absorb the experience and assimilate it to gain a greater understanding of relationships, love and self-awareness.

In a different manner to *War and Peace*, the novel *Anna Karenina* concentrates on showing the lives of the main protagonists: Anna Karenina and Konstantin Levin. Both individuals present a parallel story as they end up with different outcomes created by their actions.

The opening lines, "Happy families are all alike; every unhappy family is happy in its own way," foreshadows that there are only limited ways to be collectively happy and many reasons to be miserable.

Anna Karenina is romantically pursued by Count Vronsky and she succumbs to his love despite being married to Alexei Karenin. The reader becomes aware of Anna's actions and her inability to resist the male attention through her statement: "Love. Why I don't like the word is that it means too much for me." This is indicative of her vulnerability toward experiencing love.

The fate of Anna due to the consequence of her pursuit of love contrasts with the journey of the co-protagonist, Konstantin Levin, who is the only character who achieves a clear vision of establishing their life purpose.

Konstantin gains familial sincerity for the first time when his family is safe from a violent thunderstorm as revealed from his own reflection, "This new feeling has not changed me, has not made me happy and enlightened all of a sudden, as I had dreamed, just like the feeling for my child."

Tolstoy then shows that Konstantin realises that life's meaning is shaped by valuing the "positive meaning of goodness." By including internal monologues at key moments of Konstantin's life that contrasts the outcome of Anna's adultery, Tolstoy is able to emphasise the belief that the only way to achieve a purposeful life is to live with sincerity and gratitude.

Tolstoy, in the present time, is now regarded as one of the most prolific authors who had asserted that the nature of art carries an essential social role for society. In his book *What Is Art?*, he explores aesthetic theory and asserts that art should not only be denoted by its content in relation to the beauty or quality of fineness.

Instead, it should also take into account the significance of the experience that leads to the progressive improvement of mankind. Tolstoy states that artists should be obliged to produce art and that it can refine cultural values and benefit society as a whole.

There have been stated differences between Tolstoy's assertions on the purpose of art by other critics. Professor Gary R Jahn wrote in *The Journal of Aesthetics* and *Art Criticism* that Tolstoy's perception of art requires a moral assessment and is an incompatible criterion in the merits for evaluation of art.

It is clear that art can be interpreted from different angles and perspectives, which is the result of the myriad of reasons pertaining to its creation. While it is not required for art to be morally abiding, it is necessary for artists to recognise that their works can influence the shaping of cultures which can in turn affect individual groups and society.

Accentuating with Tolstoy's perspective of informing potential life lessons, it is through the virtue of providing positive influences through the medium of art that people and society are able to collectively improve.

Art is a medium that allows the audience to be entertained, which develops the potential of creating a group following. The attraction formed through the entertainment of art can also include knowledge that is applicable to real life.

Filmmakers can present their intended message through a script and utilisation of cinematographic techniques. In literature, authors can express their point of views through the plot combined with an assimilation of literary techniques.

Similarly, the tune, melody and lyrics of a song can also reveal an artist's intent behind the creation of a song. Within such respective contexts, artists can express their sentiments and opinions through the medium of art in a manner that is both entertaining *and* informative.

Through the experience of pleasure derived from observing, watching or listening to the arts, artists can establish a following that brings people together. It is through the commonly accepted views and beliefs that individuals form a collective group.

This can expand into the shaping of norms within the cultural standards of society. It is the collective culture that influences and can ultimately determine what people perceive as right and wrong. Thus, art can influence and shape the cultural standards of society.

Through assessing the effects of art, individuals are able to improve their ability to recognise the process by which right and wrong is commonly established. It is through the same interest that brings people together and emphasises the importance of being within the right relationships.

Genuine relationships do not only enhance what one values through the discussions of interaction, but also reinforces the certitude of belonging.

Interrelationships

Humans are social beings who benefit from the socialising elements of relationships. People interact with others in order to connect and belong through the reciprocity of established connections.

The social component of our innate nature aims to satisfy our personal means, which is correlative to the needs of another individual. However, as people gain an effective level of rapport, people will return to their relative level of equilibrium due to hedonic adaptation.

One of the following implications is that people grow dissatisfied with their circumstance and seek further levels of fulfilment whereby striving to satisfy their ego and self-esteem.

Conversely, the optimal implication after gaining rapport is that people will further the interaction that mutually benefits both parties. It is important to determine how you value your relationships so you can focus on improving the connections that are worthwhile to you.

Valuable Character Traits

A person's character trait expresses their personality, which articulates reference indicators that can determine the genuineness of one's relationships. Loyalty, sincerity and respect are distinct qualities of a person's character that can instinctively serve as a measure of the individual's amicability.

The qualities of forming such a moral character were valued throughout the course of history, including the period of Victorian Morality during the middle of the nineteenth century in Britain.

It was during that time, when society focused on the importance of truthfulness, personal responsibilities and upholding social etiquettes.

The loyalty of a person is determined by whether they are reliable and supportive throughout the course of the relationship. This is established through reflecting on the interaction between you and others, particularly during the periods when you were facing difficulties.

Furthermore, it is important to recognise a person's sincerity which is shown through their actions. To recognise that they are sincere implies integrity, mutual respect and a quality of genuineness.

Relationships benefit from the values of sincerity as they allow both parties to interact with reciprocity and the collective interest in mind. The analysis in the engagement qualities is an important factor when determining the loyalty of people.

Types of Listening

When meeting with individuals for the first or consecutive time, it can be challenging to recognise whether the person is genuinely interested in your statements and opinions. Since people at the beginning will interact with other people with the same level of etiquette, it is necessary to interact recognising their manner of listening.

How a person listens, has a significant influence on how they speak. The type of listening people apply therefore determines their type of response. As such, this evaluates the quality of the interaction and is an influential measure for determining the quality of a relationship.

1. **Critical Listening.** Involves paying attention by trying to understand and comprehend the discussion before furthering the interaction. People will use critical listening to build rapport with other individuals who can further the engagement.
2. **Appreciative listening.** Engage within the interaction to recognise and understand the perspective of others. People will use appreciative listening in order to comprehend the circumstance that potentially leads to the forming of a mutual understanding.
3. **Biased listening**. Involves listening with a particular bias, which leads to misinterpreting the conversation with an evaluation that distorts the facts or ideas in order to fit one's own intentions.
4. **Empathetic Listening**. Seeking to understand and comprehend what the other person is feeling by establishing an emotional connection.

Demonstrating empathy involves considering the other person's perspective and experiences. This can result in increasing the level of compassion between the individuals.

If a person is regularly listening and responding to you in an attentive and empathic manner, this indicates that there is a reciprocal connection within the engagement. This advocates the potential development of a relationship, which is common within close friendships and family settings.

People will generally use critical listening if they are trying to connect with other individuals in the workplace and social settings.

Individuals who engage in appreciative listening often mediate the interaction with other parties in order for all individuals to come to an agreement. These individuals are empathetic and are associated with higher degrees of conscientiousness within their personality.

Conversely, individuals who engage in biased listening experience doubt and uncertainty which is derived from their own perspective. Due to the different circumstances and a person's present frame of mind, people may also react differently within the interaction.

Through evaluating the engagements and quality of the listening, you are then able to become increasingly informed about whether the relationship coincides with your values.

Disagreements and Mutual Appreciation

Relationships will lead to interactions that result in agreements or disagreements. It is expected that people will have different perspectives and opinions with regard to a topic. When the disagreement remains unsolved, this will often lead to conflict.

Since it is inevitable to have disagreements, it is beneficial for both people in the interaction to agree to disagree. For people to disagree without the need to cause conflict or any personal animosity will benefit from such compromise fulfilled by both parties.

It is inevitable that you will experience interactions that intend to benefit one of the parties. However, the purpose of relationships is for both parties to interact, connect and build rapport while enjoying the company of other people.

If the other person disregards this mutual agreement, it is in the interests of both parties to walk away from this interaction. You will leave experiencing short-term repercussions that will be overcome by the long-term benefits of valuing other genuine relationships in the future.

This will allow you to cherish quality interactions that have mutual appreciation toward both parties. As a result, avoiding unfavourable relationships in the future will allow you to connect with other individuals who share similar values, interest and mutual reciprocity.

Determining the genuineness of relationships is essential toward maintaining the connectedness and the reciprocity for both parties. Through evaluating a person's character traits, as well as realising the type of listening and speaking that is applied and how the person responds to disagreements, you are able to determine the nature of the relationship.

Relationships that have collective interests in mind whereby combining the reciprocity of the needs of the individuals is representative of an amicable relationship. As a result, both parties are able to interact with rapport which furthers the quality of the relationship in a manner that is genuine.

Reciprocal relationships do not only engage in interactions during positive circumstances but also reinforce the sustenance of the parties during the experiences of difficult circumstances.

If the relationship is not based on the collective interests of the persons involved, this indicates that the foundations underlying the connection are not built on consistent grounds. Therefore, it will be challenging to sustain over the long term.

It is in one's interest to establish relationships based on mutual reciprocity and sincerity. This will allow you to increase your connectedness and rapport within your interactions. As a result, you will be able to enhance the beneficial relationships that further the sharing of experiences.

Debate and Discussion

Strong minds discuss ideas, average minds discuss events, weak minds discuss people.
—Socrates

Individually, people are able to conceive and refine their goals. However, people can then improve this strategy of setting objectives from the discussion of ideas. Through undertaking engagements, people are able to hear different perspectives from others which will guide them toward forming the optimal decision.

Through the reciprocated relationships, you can find credible information from those who share similar perspectives and experiences within a topic of discussion. It is through this collective nature of sharing information that leads to discussions and debates.

This interactive medium was consistently carried out by the philosopher Socrates who created his own method of cooperative debate, which was later referred to as one of his important contributions to Western philosophy.

Regarded as the first moral philosopher, Socrates from fifth century BC sought to develop a comprehensive understanding of how virtue could be obtained. Socrates sought to debate with individuals through a series of asking and answering questions in order to elicit a rational agreement.

This form of cooperative argumentative dialogue is referred to as the Socratic Method, which is used to stimulate critical thinking and remove the erroneous presumptions of an individual.

The Socratic Method is currently used by many law faculties in modern universities that have the aim of refining the students' and colleagues' understanding of legal principles.

Discussions via the Socratic Method led Socrates to conclude, that it is from the knowledge of virtue that he established how the collective elements of the good and the bad are determined.

This led the moral philosopher to establish the concept of human ethics. Socrates developed the standards for virtue ethics that guided people on how they could live a virtuous life.

The means of engagement through the use of the Socratic Method can guide people to solve many of life's questions by enhancing their perspective toward the matters and ideas that they perceive are important.

Personal interactions with other people lead to the discussion of different opinions, advice and points of view that allow you to obtain external second-hand experiences. These different perspectives offers an opportunity to observe the circumstance in another light that enhances people's ability to further the attainment of knowledge.

From the collective means of accumulating other people's experiences, you are then given the opportunity to refine your aspirations that lead to obtaining your desired results.

There are however many circumstances where you will need to rely on your own self-reliance in order to accomplish your objectives. This involves the need to plan ahead in order to achieve the desired future results.

As such, while your relationships can lead you to setting ideal objectives, you will often need to independently pursue your goals. This process of self-reliance is integral towards accomplishing your personal achievements which is exemplified from the works of Leonardo da Vinci.

Leonardo's Enhanced Perspective

Leonardo da Vinci was an Italian painter, architect, inventor and engineer whose skills represented the popular humanistic ideals of the Renaissance. Born on 15 April 1452, during the middle phase of humanistic resurgence, the disciplines of art and science were not regarded as mutually exclusive.

Instead, these fields were perceived to be complementary to one another. Modern society shows a disparity between artists and scientists as each profession focuses on their areas of expertise.

Scientists are perceived to be logical and rigorous thinkers while artists can utilise their creativity to express their skills. It is in the capabilities of both occupations that each field originally required their own methodological approach to experiment in order to find their intended results.

Leonardo da Vinci was able to pursue both the scientific and artistic fields by perceiving his own methodologies through the process of thinking ahead.

At first, Leonardo conceived of a scientific method that involved the systematic observations of the world around him before conducting an experiment that determined the causes that lead to the result.

The scientist quotes, "First I shall do some experiments before I proceed farther, because my intention is to cite experience first and then with reasoning show why such experience is bound to operate in such a way. And this is the true rule by which those who speculate about the effects of nature must proceed."

Leonardo's focus on the visual understanding of nature to use the scientific method remained pivotal in his scientific, artistic and technological discoveries.

The method Leonardo used for discovering scientific knowledge was based on his visual understanding of nature that began after starting his original career as an artist. The observation of nature and the detail to which da Vinci was able to project his artistic talents comes from his understanding that, "Painting embraces within itself all the forms of nature."

Leonardo's approach to creating art is demonstrated in his repeated expressions of emphasising the intimate connection between the artistic representation of nature and the understanding of its underlying principles. He developed many works of art including the Mona Lisa, Vitruvian Man and the Last Supper.

This systematic method may be perceived as fundamental in modern times. However, the field of science was almost devoid during the Middle Ages and it wasn't until the fourteenth century that saw the beginning of the Renaissance movement, centring upon the utilitarian approach of humanism.

Hence there were no standards for any processes of experimentation and within the conceiving of scientific principles. Leonardo established his own scientific method of collecting evidence from his experimentation before deducing reasoning from critical thinking.

By using the scientific method, Leonardo made scientific developments and new discoveries in the fields of biology, art, physics, engineering, alchemy and music.

Having studied and dissected the human body, Leonardo noted the resemblance of the symmetrical proportions that were used in ancient Roman architecture, which inspired the human proportions used in his drawing of the Vitruvian Man.

Furthermore, it was from his investigations working in the field of physiology that involved analysing bones and joints that led him to the study of the mechanics of levers and gears. This led to his sketching of the conception of the bicycle, along with the early design of the helicopter and the precursor of the modern tank.

As a result, the findings from each field enabled Leonardo to interlink human anatomy with the fields of physics and engineering.

Da Vinci's interdisciplinary foresight was established from using his own empirical method in the disciplines compared to many fields that lacked an approach toward scientific discovery. It was from his self-reliance that allowed him to think ahead and conceptualise the scientific strategy to make new discoveries.

Through his own independent approach toward developing an efficient problem-solving strategy, Leonardo consistently aimed to challenge his and others opinions to inspire creativity before developing his own discoveries.

For da Vinci, his ability to solve a myriad of life's problems included his contributions made within the fields of architecture, engineering, alchemy, physiology and human anatomy. His far-reaching contribution to society was made viable through his own dependency to view problems from another lens, resulting in new solutions.

It was through this independence stemming from his peripheral observation of nature that formed an effective strategy which led to the developments made within many interdisciplinary fields.

Now, it is not advantageous nor beneficial to replicate da Vinci, but rather it is optimal to improve your own perspectives in evaluating circumstances. It is through reinforcing one's own self-reliance that leads to the making of decisions which results in effective action.

Types of Heuristics

Our thoughts and emotions determine our perceptions. It is from this cognitive processing that helps shapes our decisions and actions. While the decisions people make often have their best intentions, the mind is subject to cognitive biases within the decision-making process.

It is common for individuals to unconsciously exacerbate the negative or positive emotions from an experience which leads to cognitive biases. An awareness of how the mind breaks down information in order to make effective decisions allows individuals to address the cognitive biases so they can refine their decisions and actions.

Heuristic is a mental shortcut that our brain uses to solve problems and make quick decisions. Everyday people make thousands of decisions, i.e., whether to undertake a certain action, believe in someone or decide how to appropriately respond to a circumstance.

Our minds employ heuristics as a mental strategy, since it would be overly strenuous for our brains to spend time thinking and analysing every piece of information. To make decisions without needing to spend a lot of time thinking and analysing information, the brain tries to simplify the decision-making process by utilising mental bypasses.

While our minds benefit from using heuristics, this process of cognition is subject to cognitive biases. Recognising the heuristics and when these cognitive biases will occur, allows people to improve their decision-making abilities.

1. Availability Heuristic

The availability heuristic is a mental shortcut that aims to make conclusions based on what the mind perceives immediately. People are subject to decisions based on the information readily available within their minds.

For example, if you tell your relatives that you are flying overseas on holiday, they may immediately respond that it is dangerous to fly in an aircraft. Because air disasters are the first thing that came to mind, the availability heuristic leads the mind to project that plane crashes are more common than what the statistics indicate.

This is similarly evident after viewing news stories of house robberies. People will perceive that the likelihood of the event is greater than previously perceived. The availability heuristic often occurs within the matters that are disturbing to the individual and which may cause detrimental effects to others or themselves.

In addition, the field of psychology has carried out research on people's abilities to remember names that are associated with fame compared with names of less fame. Psychologists Daniel Kahneman and Amos Tversky have carried out availability heuristic research where two groups were asked to listen to thirty-nine names.

One group had the list containing nineteen famous female singers and twenty *less* famous male singers. The other group were asked to recall nineteen famous male singers and twenty *less* famous female singers. The research found that 85 percent of the participants recalled a number of more famous names than less famous names.

This indicates that the ease to recall the subject, people or outcome will influence the frequency with which the circumstance occurs. As such, the initial perception that comes to mind will potentially result in the forming of cognitive biases.

Recognising when these biases occur will allow you to address and mitigate this cognitive tendency within your decision-making process.

2. Representativeness Heuristic

When faced with uncertainty in making a decision, people often rely on a mental shortcut known as the representativeness heuristic. This shortcut involves classifying the present situation with the most representative mental prototype in order to speed up the decision-making process.

There are two categories of prototypes including: 1) resemblance in prominent attributes; and 2) cause and effect. People commonly use representativeness in linking an individual's character to specific personality traits in order to determine their personality and character—i.e., a person whom you have viewed as caring and loving will be categorised in relation to your grandma who expressed similar levels of affection.

Similarly, it would be expected from the representativeness heuristic to perceive the occupation of an individual who has a high level of intelligence but is rigid in thinking and lacks creativity to be a scientist rather than other potential occupations.

The representativeness of the human mind also aims to allocate logical reasoning for the cause and effect of the implication of circumstances. For example, in finance, the price of a stock is expected to increase if it meets profit expectations in the next quarter.

However, the stock fails to rise despite achieving the forecasted outcome of this milestone. This is where the representativeness heuristic is subject to biases in reasoning. Another example of the heuristic projecting cause and effect is, when a car has broken down.

If your car has previously overheated and the incident was attributed to a radiator failure, it is expected that you will first think that your car has broken down based from the previous cause. After the mechanical diagnosis, it was revealed that the overheating was caused by a low level of coolant.

This perception of resembling circumstances and their cause and effect will result in cognitive biases to occur. However, we often do not have the time to make detailed evaluations before making choices.

By understanding the processes within the representativeness heuristics, you can be informed of potential inaccuracies in your value judgment and make optimal decisions.

3. Affect Heuristic

The affect heuristic is a type of mental shortcut whereby people make decisions based on their present frame of mind. Think of a time when individuals made decisions, based from the emotions of fear, disappointment, pleasure, surprise, etc.

The mind reacts differently to situations derived on the current emotions a person is experiencing. Research by Melissa Finucane et al., published in the

Journal of Behavioural Decision Making has found that people in a positive state of mind are more likely to perceive decisions as having higher benefits and lower risks.

On the other hand, negative emotions draw attention to the focus of the potential drawbacks rather than the possible benefits.

It is the emotional response of the human mind that influences the unconscious perceptions within the decision-making process. The conscious mind reacts to unconscious perceptions and then makes decisions. To respond in an objective manner, particularly in circumstances that manifest exacerbated sentiments requires people to regulate and discard their emotions.

Now that people are informed of their emotions, they can now introspect toward disposing the perceptions that unconsciously trigger the root cause. This will allow individuals to obtain an equilibrium state of mind and as a result, they will form clarity within their decision-making process.

Through being aware of heuristics and cognitive processing, you can enhance the knowledge of your self-awareness. The realisation of the availability of thoughts, representativeness between prototypes and the effect of sentiments are strategies for individuals to make mental shortcuts within their decision-making processes.

By reducing the mental burden required in the mind, you are then able to make quick and accurate decisions. Now that you are aware of heuristics, this will allow you to recognise when to utilise and evaluate mental shortcuts.

As a result, you can refine the consistency in making accurate decisions that lead to optimal outcomes.

Key Points

1. The access to information and knowledge are now widely available. However, the ideal perspectives are often neglected.
2. For people to enhance their perspective involves valuing the importance of the effects in matters such that they are able to improve the processes to think and achieve ahead.
3. Art offers not only an experience from the dimension of its beauty, but it also connects people with similar interests that has the potential to collectively influence and shape the cultures of society.
4. Leo Tolstoy was able to produce literary works that consistently invited readers to immerse within his character's experiences, portraying the reasoning and outcome of their actions.
5. Any medium that influences society as a whole is required to undertake a conscious assessment from the developer pertaining to its creation.
6. The collective assessment of what people perceive as right and wrong are shaped by the cultural norms of society.
7. Relationships, when reciprocated with authenticity, increases the mutual reciprocity and connectedness between both parties that furthers the sharing of desirable experiences.
8. Interacting in debates and discussion elicits critical thinking and the stimulation of creativity to derive viable solutions to matters.
9. Socrates used the Socratic Method to elicit rational outcomes that led to forming the standard of virtue ethics, which guided people to live with integrity.
10. Beyond the benefit of collective interactions from the refining of objectives, enhancing one's own perspectives also requires the self-reliance of independent planning and execution.
11. Leonardo da Vinci solved a myriad of life's problems through establishing the scientific method that allowed him to further his ability to make discoveries through various interdisciplinary fields.
12. While people make decisions using their best interpretations, the mind remains subject to biases.
13. There are three types of common heuristics including the availability, representativeness and affect heuristic.

14. Through being aware of heuristics, you are able to refine your ability to make quick and accurate decisions. As a result, you are able to carry out effective actions that are aligned towards achieving optimal results.

Chapter 7
Emphasise Your Belief System

The increase in the rights and freedom within the twenty-first century has allowed people to believe in what they decide to believe in. We are now able to shape our own identities by pursuing the actions that we believe are best for our personal interests.

This has resulted in the rise of consumerism, nihilism and the decline of religiousness within cultures. However, many popular belief systems currently do not associate with living an optimistic and fulfilled life.

This chapter explores Stoic philosophy and examines the motivations of human need so you can reinforce your own belief systems. From establishing a robust foundation that underpins your own self-worth, you are then able to certify your ability to self-actualise.

The Philosophical Movement of Stoicism

Zeno of Citium born in 334 BC initially became a wealthy merchant. On a voyage trading goods from Peiraeus to Phoenicia, he was shipwrecked close to his arrival destination.

He survived while his ship sank along with its cargo. Zeno coasted toward the city of Athens and entered a bookstall. There, he encountered the second book of Xenophon's *Memorabilia*, which gave practical advice regarding the philosophical views of Socrates.

Zeno developed an interest in the contents of the book, which led him to inquire where such men as described in the book lived. Crates of Thebes, who was a known Cynic philosopher, happened to pass by the bookstore and the clerk pointed to him.

Zeno became a devoted learner of philosophy and began to adhere to the principles of Cynicism, where the principles outlined the purpose of life was to live with virtue and in accordance with nature.

The essence of human life was perceived by the Cynics to focus on freedom and self-sufficiency. This involved rejecting the desires of fame, power, sex and wealth since the Cynics lived free of all possessions.

However, over time, the former merchant was unable to live under the Cynic frugality and began studying the Megarian school of philosophy. Founded in fifth century BC, the Megarian perspective had an ethical and educational purpose focusing on what was conceived as the moral good.

Based on the works of the philosopher Socrates and the Eleatic doctrine of Unity, the Megarian philosophy reinforced that virtue is gained through knowledge, and that the definition of moral good differed depending on its basis of reason, mindfulness and wisdom.

Zeno later studied other philosophers, including the Dialecticians Diodorus Cronus and Philo of Magara.

With a developed foundation of philosophy established through the research of knowledge and its application, Zeno began developing his own philosophical beliefs. In Athens, under the Stoa Poikilê (referred to as Painted Porche), Zeno taught Stoicism, which became a school of Hellenistic philosophy that aimed to improve one's self-control and detachment from unwarranted emotions without the experience of discontentment.

The philosopher recognised from his own experience that human life is often unpredictable, and by teaching Stoic philosophy, it would remind people of what they are able to control and not control. Stoicism therefore focuses on teaching the advancement of people's thoughts, beliefs, attitudes and the individual mindset.

It is perceived from Stoic principles that by obtaining virtue through reason and knowledge, people can live in accordance with nature. For the next several centuries, Stoic philosophy was taught in both Greek and Roman societies. Notable Stoic philosophers include Seneca, Epictetus and the emperor Marcus Aurelius.

Now that I've suffered shipwreck, I'm on a good journey.
—Zeno of Citium

Existing Belief Systems

The twenty-first century offers the opportunity for people to define their own set of beliefs and those shapes how they perceive their circumstances and the wider society. The shift toward a technological world has altered society's standard toward people's roles and responsibilities. It is through a person's perception of their circumstances that leads to the shaping of their belief system.

Three centuries before the 21st century, during the preindustrial revolution, a majority of the population had limited knowledge of the belief systems they should reinforce. A majority of the population, living in agriculture and farming, did not have access to books, information or knowledge.

Women were predominantly responsible for household and domestic duties while men had the responsibility of providing food and income for the exchange of goods. If people's lives had offered consistent food and stability, then it was anticipated that they lived with a positive outlook.

On the other hand, if famine, drought or instabilities occurred, it was anticipated that people lived pessimistically. It was from these circumstances that established how people lived their lives, which shaped the beliefs on their interpretations of the world.

Unlike these historical periods where the gender roles were rigid, technology has enabled the growth in the flexibility of the workforce, which increased the opportunities for both men and women. Now, we are able to pursue interests and careers that are within our personal alignment.

The shift in the current social construct resulted in the access of everyday freedoms. People have been allowed to find their purpose through their careers and aspirations. However, people who have not been aware of or are reluctant to change their current circumstances may have experienced the loss of fortuity in finding their desired motivations.

This has resulted in the conflict of differences regarding what is viewed as socially accepted. Despite an increase in the opportunities for people to pursue their purpose, it is each person's own belief system that has a significant effect on whether they will focus on the opportunities or the unfavourable aspects of their life.

It is from the shaping of a person's belief system that influences their outlook on life. Globalisation and technologies have facilitated the growth of the availability of goods and services as an increasing amount of individuals are now drawn to the experience of materialism and the outlook of increasingly positive experiences.

This trend toward materialism has increased over the years that has influenced the decline in the following of religious beliefs.

Furthermore, with the recent coronavirus pandemic that has affected people's livelihood, and combined with the trend of rising polarization between the groups in society such as the divide between the political left and right have caused the disparity between people's perceptions and reality.

As a result, this causes cognitive dissonance whereby individuals experience conflict with what do and believe in. When people consistently experience negative circumstances and remain uncertain in their values of belief, this leads to nihilism.

Nihilism is the belief that everything that once held value is now baseless and denies the meaningful aspects of life.

Nevertheless, all belief systems that we decide to believe in are arguable in nature. This is reinforced as the German philosopher Fedrick Nietzsche states that, "Every belief, every considering something-true, is necessarily false because there is simply no true world."

This statement implies that both our beliefs and underlying belief systems are determined by what we *choose* to believe in. Hence, it is from our belief system that we establish the ability to abide by our consciousness when it is in alignment with what we aspire towards.

Our belief systems are expected to change as a result of particular experiences and through the actions of carrying out reflections, contemplations and realisations. To shape a belief system that aligns with a person's personality traits, is to act in accordance with their human consciousness.

This allows people to remain compassionate towards themselves and others. Refining the belief systems you undertake allows you to coincide with your individual self.

From new knowledge, people often change their own belief systems throughout their lives. Since the world we live in is unpredictable and constantly changing, people will benefit from the assimilation of Stoic philosophy.

Stoic principles offer the ability to focus on living proactively through utilising one's own self-control in order to develop the knowledge of virtue. This will allow individuals to focus on what they can control so they can have a consistently optimistic outlook.

Beliefs of Stoicism

Direct Your Focus on What You can Control

If you are pained by any external thing, it is not this thing that disturbs you, but your own judgment about it. And it is in your power to wipe out this judgment.
—Marcus Aurelius

While you cannot change the circumstances and outcomes that are not within your control, you can change how you respond, or do not respond to the circumstance. This Stoic principle outlines that if your mind does not emotionally react to the problem, then you do not perceive there is a problem.

Recognising this will guide you toward alleviating stress and uncertainties. Establishing this mentality predisposes unnecessary beliefs and directs the attention toward what people can control.

The Obstacles You Face are an Opportunity that Leads to Advancement

When something threatens to cause you pain: the thing itself was no misfortune at all; to endure it and prevail is great good fortune.
—Marcus Aurelius

Adversity is perceived in Stoic nature as a trial and an opportunity for individuals to grow. To overcome the challenges, Stoics would turn toward themselves using knowledge, reason and inner strength. As such, the difficulties people experience offer the ability to reinforce their practice toward self-discipline.

For the Stoics, their objective to live in accordance with nature requires the need to face, endure and prevail over the challenges. People who apply this principle in the facing of obstacles are able to improve their ability to obtain inner tranquillity.

Act in Accordance with Ethical Principles

> Let all your efforts be directed to something, let it keep that end in view. It's not activity that disturbs people, but false conceptions of things that drive them mad.
>
> —Seneca

Stoics aim to establish virtue as a means to rationalise their reasoning in order to live effectively. To act with clear judgment is to base your actions on the foundations of knowledge, understanding and reason. This is based off the four cardinal virtues in Stoic philosophy that include:

1. Practical wisdom. Navigate through circumstances in a composed and informed manner.
2. Fortitude. Facing circumstances to be unmoved by fear and to act with courage and perseverance.
3. Temperance. Exercising restraint on human impulses and attaining moderation through the practice of self-control.
4. Justice. Treating others with fairness even when one has acted wrong.
5. Distinguish between the good, bad and the indifferents.

The Stoics defined *the good* as the capability to attain perfect virtue through knowledge and reason. It is perceived by following through with ethical actions that individuals experience contentment. On the other hand, it is from the corruption of reason that results in misery, namely through the acts of indiscretion, cowardice, intemperance and injustice.

The forming of these vices is recognised to be caused by the effects of confused and misinformed judgments that detract from living a fulfilled life.

Every other element that is neither beneficial nor prejudicial is classified in the category of indifferents. This term is derived from the belief that these elements neither contribute to nor detract from living a fulfilled life. Preferred indifferents consist of non-moral benefits including life, health, beauty, popularity, technical ability, wealth and reputation.

The unpreferred indifferents include death, illness, pain, unpopularity, lack of technical knowledge, poverty and a lack of repute. While it is natural for people to avoid the unpreferred indifferents, it is also occasionally virtuous to select them rather than avoid them.

This allows individuals to face adversity in order to further their ability of building resilience. As a result, Stoics believe that the unpreferred and preferred indifferents may be pursued within moderation as it is from the attainment of experience and knowledge that aligns with the path of a fulfilled life.

Being Appreciative in Your Actions

Do not indulge in dreams of having what you have not, but reckon up the chief of the blessings you do possess and then thankfully remember how you would crave for them if they were not yours.

—Marcus Aurelius

The Stoic focuses on the need to appreciate what you are currently in possession of rather than continuously seeking what you can obtain. Recognising that people are not in control of their circumstances and what they can externally acquire, this Stoic principle focuses on the mindset of individuals to establish gratitude for what they already have.

Practice the Values and Embody Them

Don't explain your philosophy. Embody it.

—Epictetus

Stoicism focuses on utilising discipline as a means of applying its principles throughout life. Through carrying out the actions of these beliefs, the Stoics can focus on the development of their personal growth which allows for this belief system to be embraced and shared among others.

The Stoic principles accentuate a dimension of knowledge relating to the fundamental interpretation of the human experience. Centring upon the human ethics of rational reasoning, Stoic principles establish a code of conduct that guides people to refine their moral self-worth.

It is through the discipline of the human mind that the Stoic directs attention toward their acts of virtue. To moderate and control human impulses, Stoic philosophy marks the importance of gratitude through the assimilation of what people have already attained.

As a result, this reduces the effects of hedonic adaptation, which allows individuals to empathise with their consciousness in a fair and justly manner. By recognising the adversities as opportunities to grow, this prepares people with the ability to navigate through challenging circumstances.

In modern psychology, Professor Emeritus Aaron Beck and Albert Ellis took inspiration from Stoic philosophers, including Epictetus and Marcus Aurelius in developing their own methods of cognitive restructuring techniques.

Respectively, the two scientists developed the Cognitive Therapy and Rational Emotive Behaviour Therapy which notably contributed to the development of Cognitive Behavioural Therapy (CBT).

The Stoic doctrine "to live in accordance with nature" can be interpreted differently and has been met with modern criticism from people of different fields.

This ethic may have been purposefully defined ambiguously as the human experience of life is also filled with open uncertainties. Furthermore, such doctrine may intend to be ambiguous, as it fosters the need for people to acknowledge and then utilise their abilities gathered from their experiences to fulfil their objectives.

While adopting the principles of Stoicism requires effort, people can benefit fundamentally from Stoic philosophy by applying the principles that are most viable for them. To recognise the areas where individuals can focus their beliefs and action leads to the trajectory toward pursuing virtue such that one can live a fulfilled life.

The Stoic Marcus Aurelius has been notably recognised by modern leaders including Bill Clinton and Nelson Mandela. In summary, Stoic philosophy provides a moral belief system that allows people to be increasingly informed of their abilities such that they can channel their energies toward attaining self-fulfilment.

The analysis of the existing, and stoic beliefs systems reveal that people's very own credence are influenced by how they can meet their needs and desires. By identifying the motivations of human needs, you are able to shift your personal obligations toward pursuing the objectives that is in alignment towards self-actualisation.

The Motivations for Human Needs

People strive to attain what they fundamentally need, followed by what they desire. It is in human nature that we unconsciously set our expectations which guides us to achieve progress. Through the behavioural conditioning of hedonic adaptation that this human process drives people to pursue their objectives that furthers their purpose.

The accumulated pursuits of fulfilling human objectives over the last thousands of years, has resulted in the improvements of the objectives people are able to pursue. This is shown in Figure 12 that presents the motivation of human needs.

Figure 12–The Motivations of Human Needs

The essential human qualities as shown in the bottom encirclement have been less challenging to obtain for many people in the twenty-first century. This is due to the increased period of peace and order combined with technological improvements which have enhanced the ability for people to obtain food, shelter, safety and security.

As people meet their essential human qualities, they will then aim to enhance their human qualities.

Enhancing human qualities include validation and interconnectedness, along with the need to further their self-esteem and self-actualisation. Self-actualisation is the human quality that allows a person to live in alignment by fulfilling their potential.

This means that through a person's fundamental self-awareness, they can achieve their needs and objectives that are in alignment with their individuality. Through refining the person's own belief system, they will then shift toward pursuing commitments that will allow them to self-actualise.

Since it has been less challenging for people to meet their essential human qualities, some individuals may decide to focus their attention on increasing their interconnectedness and validation. Validation can be obtained in the external and internal forms and people may consistently strive to accomplish this need.

From pursuing such enhanced human quality, individuals are able to benefit from the increase in rapport and connectedness. However, the predicament is that the long-term benefits obtained from external connectedness are limited due to hedonic adaptation.

Hence there should be a balance to which people should allocate in their efforts of pursuing external interconnectedness.

Alternatively, other people may increase their level of ego and self-esteem. To increase one's self-esteem requires the need to be comfortable with their individual self. It is optimal for people to improve their self-esteem by improving their own confidence and self-belief.

Conversely, individuals may also raise their own level of ego to improve their own self-esteem. This is not beneficial toward their self-worth as increasing one's ego results in undermining the position of others which deteriorates relationships.

As a result, it is necessary to build self-esteem through confidence and self-belief such, that one can fulfil their human needs without compromising their own or others.

All of our actions are associated with meeting our obligations, which require satisfying the components of our human needs. The needs revolving around family and friends centre upon belonging and interconnectedness. Conversely, the issues revolving around ego and self-esteem are centred upon the need to improve one's self-worth.

The predicaments revolving around our occupation influence our ability to obtain food, shelter and security. To self-actualise centres upon the pursuit of the ideal commitments that lead to fulfilling people's potential.

Individuals who focus on obtaining materialistic needs gain temporary comforts and external validation. However, to attain consistent levels of validation also requires the need to obtain their own internal validation. This requires people to reinforce their own values that will further their self-reliance.

As a result, obtaining external and internal validation allows people to have their own confidence in their own beliefs while also benefiting from the connectedness of relationships.

When individuals have acquired one of the needs components, it is originally deemed contrary if that person were to relinquish it. For example, if an individual belonged to a group where the other members began to consistently criticise others in order to gain external validation, the individual would become aware of this and may decide to leave the group.

However, leaving a group and potentially losing their state of belonging can prove difficult. This is because, from recalling the research of Behavioural Scientist Kelly Goldsmith and Economist Ravi Dhar, people are motivated to avoid losses more than they are to obtain an equivalent gain.

In cognitive psychology, this is referred to as loss aversion, which explains that people will place higher value on what they currently possess than if they had not yet attained it. Therefore, it is beneficial for people to belong and obtain self-esteem through the optimal means.

In analysing the motivations of human needs, to remain optimistic in the facing of difficulty through having a positive future outlook moderates negative biases. This forms a positive belief system that despite any circumstance people will face, they will be able to remain pursuing their objectives in a state of peace.

As a result, being optimistic reinforces the willingness to overcome difficulties so that people can focus on living in the present.

In summary, once people's essential human qualities have been acquired, they will then be able to focus on fulfilling the needs that result in personal development. Nevertheless, not all enhancing human qualities are optimal to pursue.

From your confidence and self-belief, you are then able to recognise the values that shape your own self-worth. With a robust foundation in your belief system, you can then pursue the commitments that result in self-actualisation.

Key Points

1. The increase in rights and freedoms of modern society has allowed people to decide what they want to believe in. People now have the opportunity to broaden their beliefs, resulting in undertaking the actions they perceive best.
2. Zeno of Citium became devoted to practicing many philosophies in order to improve his ability to live a better life after experiencing a shipwreck.
3. Stoic philosophy articulates the practice of reason to exercise self-control, fortitude and abstinence from involuntary pleasures in order to objectivise and overcome difficulties.
4. The six principles of Stoicism aim to focus on directing people to what they are able to control such that they can face obstacles and practice virtue toward experiencing preferred and unpreferred indifferents with gratitude from what they have already obtained.
5. People who practice Stoicism are able to disregard what they are unable to control so that they will be better prepared for adversity to live a fulfilled life.
6. In the twenty-first century, there has been an increasing trend toward materialism and the outlook of increasingly optimal experiences.
7. Each and every person's belief system is determined by what they decide to believe in.
8. To refine a belief system that aligns with your personality traits is to examine and act in accordance with your consciousness.
9. People consistently pursue what they need, followed by what they desire.
10. The motivation for human needs consists of the essential and enhancing human qualities, which drive people to pursue their aspired need components.
11. Self-actualisation refers to the ability for a person to live in alignment and fulfil their potential.
12. When people have been able to obtain the essential human qualities, they will then strive toward pursuing enhancing human qualities.
13. The pursuit of materialism leads to the temporary improvement of one's external validation and self-esteem.

14. It is optimal to obtain the human need components including self-esteem and validation through undertaking personal growth.
15. Loss aversion is referred to in cognitive psychology as the tendency for people to prefer avoiding losses than to acquire an equivalent gain.
16. Optimism allows people to form a belief system that moderates their negative bias such that can fulfil their obligations in a state of peace.
17. From emphasising your own set of personal values, you can then focus on aligning your consciousness to the commitments that result in self-actualisation.

Chapter 8
How to Remain Content

How to be satisfied with who you are is a question we all consistently ask ourselves. It is through your personal advancements that allow you to perceive, believe and self-actualise. But for a person to remain content requires the need to be conscious of the implications of their actions.

This involves making decisions that have a utilitarian benefit toward society. On the other hand, decisions that rebut your ethical morals lead to future regrets. By acting in accordance with your consciousness, you are able to articulate certainty in your actions and live in contentment.

This chapter provides the strategy to broaden your assessment of situations from using the Third-Person Analysis. From the refining of people's conscience, they are then able to have gratitude and appreciate living in the present.

> There is only one good, knowledge and one evil, ignorance.
> —Socrates

Knowledge has been fundamental to our survival for millions of years. From the beginning, knowledge for humans came in different forms, from developing hunting skills to finding the means for navigation. Throughout the millennia, we have been able to improve our ability to gain knowledge due to increased access to information.

The willingness to learn has resulted in the population becoming more educated and informed in academic disciplines. Now, if the population had reversed its view toward the importance of attaining knowledge, this would cause conflict within the cultural standards that would affect what actions would be perceived as acceptable.

Philosophy is the study of the fundamental questions regarding how knowledge derives the reasoning and value of human existence. To solve these philosophical questions, neuroscientists, psychologists and philosophers aim to direct individuals with the reasons to establish the ideal course of action.

It is from our ability to obtain philosophical knowledge that allows people to act with conscious intentions, while others decide to act otherwise.

The moral philosopher Socrates outlines that good can only be attained through knowledge. In his teachings of virtue, Socrates explains that people who act with bad intentions attain those same desires that are perceived to be good, but it is carried out in a contradictory manner.

For example, if one person threatens another person, they aim to gain power that leads to the experience of temporary pleasures by validating their ego. However, this is at the expense of going against their conscience and upon self-reflection, it will result in discontentment.

An immoral act that is perceived to be good carries the unconscious guilt that outweighs the gains. The person who experiences the reaction to the unvirtuous deed does not in fact experience the impediment as much as the perpetrator.

It is the development of guilt that leads to the disrepute of a person's conscience which lowers their self-esteem.

The motives that result in immoral behaviours are often derived from the means of striving to gain power, wealth, lust and pleasure. This does not indicate that such means are not to be pursued, but that these indifferences should be derived as a result of reinforcing an individual's moral sense of purpose.

For example, to obtain wealth, as tentatively defined is to be acquired only from making a positive difference toward others and themselves. Correspondingly, pleasure is to be experienced as a result of pursuing one's needs and desires on the condition that it does not cause any negative implications toward other people.

It is necessary for people to be aware of the effects of their conducts such that they are able to remain content. To navigate in according to one's moral conscience had been exemplified by Nelson Mandela, who despite difficulties, remained devoted toward advocating equal rights and opportunities for every person in South Africa.

Nelson Mandela's Path to Presidency

Nelson Mandela was a South African political leader who led the movement toward ending racial segregation and unified the South African communities together for the maintenance of peace. The path for Nelson to accomplish these social developments would not be obtained before facing many moral challenges.

Born in 1918, Mandela was brought up in a South African society where racism among the native South Africans, mixed races and white South Africans (predominantly Dutch, British, German and French settlers) was common.

While studying for a Bachelor of Arts degree at the University College of Fort Hare, Mandela became a student representative and participated in a protest against university policies. The university gave him an ultimatum to either remain part of the student council or he would be forced to disenroll in the university.

Sticking to his conscience, he would return home and upon his arrival, the regent of his community ordered him to return to the university or he would be forced into a formally arranged marriage.

Sticking to his principles and dismayed by such a proposal, Mandela fled to Johannesburg. There, he found work as a mine security officer and was later introduced to Walter Sisulu who was an activist for the African National Congress (ANC).

The ANC aimed to bring all South African citizens together to stop racism which would advocate toward national liberation. It was Sisulu who helped Mandela secure a job as an article clerk at the law firm Witkin, Sidelsky and Eidelman.

Mandela later signed up to study at the University of South Africa via correspondence and worked on his bachelor's degree at night. Graduating in 1943, Mandela then joined the ANC where he helped form the ANC Youth League.

After the 1948 elections, the South African government, under the new rule of the National Party, adopted a new racial segregation policy called apartheid. Referred in the West Germanic language Afrikaans as 'apartness,' this policy was responsible for the native Africans, mixed race and the white South African populations to live separately.

Furthermore, the apartheid laws also dictated employment opportunities while mandating racial segregation within schools, social events and the use of public facilities such that contact among the races remained limited.

Mandela had remained a committed member of the ANC, and by 1949 he was raised in rank and elected to its board of the National Executive Committee. The organisation adopted a radical-based policy referred to as the 'Programme of Action,' which was proactive toward opposing apartheid by embarking on mass action.

This included organising a series of work strikes, boycotts, civil disobedience and other forms of nonviolent resistance. In 1952, the ANC and the South African Indian Congress prepared a joint Defiance Campaign that promoted the strategy of using nonviolent resistance which was pursued by joint groups.

During the same year, at a rally held in the city of Durban on June 22 with a crowd of 10,000, Mandela was later arrested for his role in the Defiance Campaign and was placed in Marshall Square Prison. Mandela was among one of the twenty-one members charged with opposing the apartheid laws.

He was found guilty and sentenced to nine months of hard labour, which was suspended with probation for a period of two years.

Mandela with his limited freedom was banned for a period of six months from attending meetings and addressing more than one person at a time. With ongoing protests in opposition to apartheid, the ANC membership grew during 1952 and rose from 20,000 to over 100,000 members.

This was followed with the South African government's response regarding opposition to the apartheid laws by introducing the Public Safety Act in 1953. This policy empowered the South African government to declare stringent emergencies that would enable any means, including that of military intervention to uphold the law.

Also evident in this act was the increase in penalties for protesting against or supporting the repeal of the law. The apartheid laws remained fiercely contested for decades to come.

In 1955, during the forced relocation of all native African citizens in the suburb of Sophiatown, Mandela was involved in protests that proved unsuccessful. That is when he concluded that in order to end apartheid, other forms of resistance were no longer open that would result in an armed struggle.

During this period, the government intensified the banning of ANC members. Collaborating with other congresses and trade unions, the ANC formed an assembly that called on South African citizens to send their proposals for a post-apartheid era.

This document is known as the Freedom Charter that called for human rights, labour rights, land reforms and nationalisation of public assets. By September 1955, the South African government banned forty-eight of its members including Mandela from the ANC.

In the following year, Mandela received a subsequent ban, restricting him from returning to Johannesburg for five years.

Mandela was arrested on December 5, 1956, alongside other ANC national executives and employees of *The Guardian* newspaper on the act of treason against the state. A total of 156 people were jailed in Johannesburg Prison before proceeding with what is known as the Treason Trial.

While the accused underwent a preparatory examination, mass protests erupted in reaction to the trial. The following day, bail was granted for the defendants and court proceedings restarted in January 1957.

While Mandela remained on trial during the year of 1960, a protest took place in Sharpeville where police fired weapons and killed sixty-nine unarmed citizens while also wounding 186 others.

The demonstrators retaliated against this incident by carrying out protest marches and strikes throughout the country. This led to South Africa's first state of emergency. The government received international controversy as the United Nations Security Council intervened in South African affairs for the first time.

This incident resulted in the South African government pre-emptively banning the ANC while many of its leaders remained on trial. This court case continued for four years until 29 March 1961 and all the defendants including Mandela were found not guilty and were acquitted.

Chief Luthuli, a future Nobel Peace Prize winner, referred to the treason trial as a deliberate predawn raid used to strike terror and impress upon the entire nation that the government would stifle all opposition to apartheid by charging the accused with one of the most serious charges in the legal system.

By 1962, many of the anti-apartheid activists resorted to violence and Mandela believed the ANC should organise a controlled armed struggle for a non-apartheid cause. To raise support, Mandela travelled to England and across Africa while also receiving demolition and mortar training.

Returning to South Africa after a month, Mandela briefed the plans of his trip with the ANC and discussed future strategies. During a police roadblock on 5 August 1962, Mandela was arrested outside the town of Harwick situated in Eastern South Africa.

Charged with leaving the country without a permit and citing worker strikes, Mandela intended to use the trial to showcase the ANC's moral opposition to racism. Mandela concluded that no matter the outcome that awaited him, he would remain committed to the struggle for a post-apartheid future. Mandela was found guilty and sentenced to five years in prison.

While Mandela was in jail and during a police raid on an ANC hideout in Rivonia, quantities of arms and equipment were found. Mandela, along with ten other leading individuals opposing apartheid, was tried for sabotage in 1962 in what was known as the Rivonia Trial.

Mandela and five other individuals admitted to sabotage but denied any attempts to initiate war against the government. At the beginning of the defence proceedings, Mandela gave a three-hour "I Am Prepared to Die" speech as he faced the death penalty.

At the concluding statement of his speech, Mandela stated: "During my lifetime I have dedicated my life to this struggle of the African people. I have cherished the ideal of a democratic and free society in which all people will live together in harmony and with equal opportunities. It is an ideal for which I hope to live for and to see realised. But, my Lord, if it needs to be, it is an ideal for which I am prepared to die." Nelson Mandela was convicted of sabotage and sentenced to life in prison.

On the eleventh year after his arrest, the South African government offered Mandela a conditional release in which he would be required to confine in the state of Transkei of where he was originally born.

Mandela declined this offer due to the limitation imposed on his activity of movement and freedom of speech. Throughout the years, the South African government periodically presented different offers of conditional release, which he would consistently decline.

Mandela remained outspoken in challenging the apartheid laws while recognising that it would not be beneficial for the terms of his release.

By the 1980s, South Africa became increasingly isolated in international trade relations and sporting events due to the lack of developments made in human rights relations. This decade saw an increase in protests, strikes and armed struggle.

The South African government implemented the Tricameral parliament in 1984 that gave new limited political power to the mixed coloured and Indian population groups but neglected the native African population.

In response, this was opposed by the United Democratic Front (UDF) that included a coalition of 400 entities of trade unions and faith-based organisations. In the inception of the UDF, more than 13,000 people gathered together, which was the largest anti-racial gathering since the 1950s.

By 1985, supporters for the UDF grew to 1.5 million people. With an increasing number of protests, violence had escalated, and the government responded by increasing repression, which increased the conflict throughout the country.

Bilateral negotiations to secretly end apartheid commenced during 1987 as the National Party faced increasing external pressures. During this time period, equality in rights and opportunities had since become increasingly prevalent throughout the rest of the world.

Leading ANC officials were beginning to be released after 1987. On 11 February 1990, South African President Frederik Willem de Klerk released Nelson Mandela after serving twenty-seven years in prison. On the day of Mandela's release, he addressed the crowd outlining his focus to end apartheid.

The banning of the ANC was lifted while Mandela and de Klerk both focused on the peaceful transition toward developing equitable social and political systems. In 1993, Mandela and de Klerk both received the Nobel Peace Prize for the peaceful termination of the apartheid regime.

Nelson Mandela was elected as the South African president in 1994. As president, Mandela was responsible for the national reconciliation of human rights and established a council to acknowledge the previous violations. These policies were directed for the citizens of South Africa to find peace and solidarity so that the nation could direct its focus towards promoting social unity and prosperity.

One of the most difficult things is not to change society but to change yourself.
—Nelson Mandela

Nelson Mandela is a figure who was able to foresee that all individuals deserve equal rights and opportunities. During the twenty-seven years Mandela served in prison, his credence for a non-apartheid future for his country remained consistent.

Even though the National Party attempted to silence him, Mandela remained disciplined and withstood the pressure which had furthered his cause. Although

Mandela remained a private person, a letter from the former president confiding with his former wife in prison after thirteen years of his final sentence showed him reciting the importance of, "Honesty, sincerity, simplicity, humility, pure generosity, absence of vanity, readiness to serve others—qualities which are within easy reach of every soul— are the foundation of one's spiritual life."

It was through acting in accordance with his own conscience that Mandela reinforced his ability to remain determined in not only ending apartheid, but also in uniting the country to establish a multiracial government.

At the start of his presidency in 1994, Mandela faced significant challenges as the nation began transitioning into a multiracial country. The previous violations to human rights could have been subject to prosecution, however, this would only cause embitterment among the various communities.

Instead, Mandela established The Truth and Reconciliation Commission (TRC) in 1996 that was tasked with revealing the past acts of wrongdoing by previous individuals, organisations and government entities.

The restorative court-modelled justice gave victims the ability to be heard at the TRC proceedings, which would release their distress and anger and that resulted in the forming of solidarity. The perpetrators were also given the ability to explain their actions in request for amnesty.

Through implementing the practice of consolation on a national scale, this addressed the afflictions caused by the previous tensions which resulted in the South African communities to unite.

Mandela developed many policies that strived to improve equality, welfare and education while reinforcing the peace of the South Africans for the then present, and future generations. Mandela's ability to settle racial tensions on a national scale was reflected in his competence for being able to express and deliberate his compassion to forgive and then persevere.

Through living in alignment to his own conscience, this reinforced the former president's ability to unite and direct the South African nation toward peace and freedom.

In analysing Nelson Mandela's path to presidency, it is clear that he had faced countless moral challenges. The former president's dedication to obtain equal rights and opportunities for all South African citizens was developed from his own certainty towards what he had perceived as righteous from a utilitarian perspective.

Utilitarian Third-Person Analysis

Utilitarianism is a moral theory that determines the right and wrong based on outcomes of choosing one action over another. The philosophy of utilitarianism outlines that the most ethical course of action is the one that results in the highest accumulation of utility which can be referred to as the benefit, advantage and the good for the most amount of people.

There are two different forms of utilitarianism—rule and act utilitarianism. These respectively focus on the requirement to follow rules and undertake the actions that maximise the utility of outcomes.

The purpose of utilitarian ethics is for people, where possible to undertake action that benefits other people as well as themselves.

It is optimal for people to analyse the circumstances that they regard as important, including their career, interests and passion of whether they offer a utilitarian benefit. As the objectives will change over time, it will become an inconvenience to analyse each separate circumstance that takes into account the stakeholder's impact. This is where it is effective to utilise the Third-Person Analysis.

The Third-Person Analysis involves widening the perspective of analysing the consequences of potential actions such that people will become comprehensively informed before making decisions.

This strategy utilises a third-person perspective in assessing the situation that includes other people's points of view in addition to your own. As a result, you will then be informed to undertake the actions that benefit others as well as yourself.

Figure 13–Third-Person Analysis vs Limited Perspective

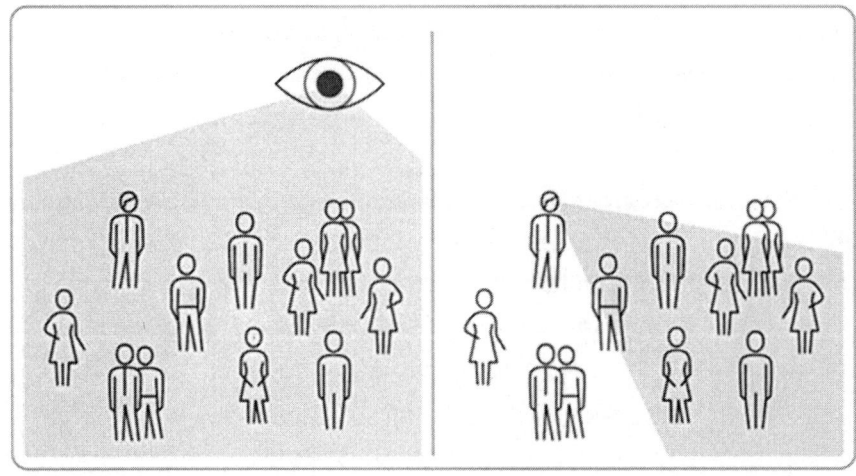

Analysing the intended and unintended effects before undertaking the action expands your comprehensiveness to make accurate decisions. These impacts, when undertaking the course of action, informs you of the inadvertent effects of indecency, moral righteousness or an effect that is negligible.

By being able to analyse a situation in a comprehensive manner, people can minimise their regrets. When a decision has the potential to significantly affect other people or society, it is optimal to undertake the third-person perspective as it brings clarity to make conscious decisions.

In utilising the Third-Person Analysis for analysing Nelson Mandela's path, it is clear that his actions were aimed at providing equal rights, opportunities and equality for all South African citizens. Through establishing fairness toward every ethnicity, this incentivised the ethnic communities to unite peacefully which would prove salutary to the South African nation.

On the opposing side of Mandela's cause, were individuals who attempted to condemn him which supported apartheid and racial segregation. This perspective toward increasing the seclusion among the communities advocated intolerance, segregation and mistreatment among the different races.

From a third-person perspective of analysing which representative case is most utilitarian, it is evident that a society with equal rights and opportunities among all citizens would advocate toward peace and acceptance.

It is through this course of action that Nelson Mandela was able to unilaterally lead as president and implement reforms that established solidarity throughout different communities. As a result, Nelson Mandela was then able to focus on promoting socioeconomic developments that furthered the prosperity of South Africa.

It is optimal to use the third-person perspective in matters that have the potential to significantly impact other people or society at large.

There are also less prominent actions that are common and habitual which can have an accumulated effect on others. This can include the need for people to interact with other people on a daily basis. Since people's actions are refined once they are consciously aware, a Third-Person Analysis can be beneficial in establishing certainty in their decision-making.

Nevertheless, it is impossible to always satisfy the interests of other people. The intention of using the Third-Person Analysis strategy is to carry out the actions that have a utilitarian benefit toward others and oneself where possible.

Therefore, for the matters that have a potentially significant impact would benefit from undertaking an extensive analysis, whereas limited effecting matters can be repudiated.

As a result, people are able to focus their attention on the objectives based on their degree of importance.

Hence, this strategy can be suggested for others or yourself to obtain certainty in determining the outcome of major decisions.

In summary, using the Third-Person Analysis allows people to develop a comprehensive outlook that refines their decision-making abilities. This strategy of taking oneself and others into consideration will allow you to contribute utilitarian benefits to society.

Through enhancing yours or other people's ability to make effective decisions, this reduces one's potential to experience future regrets. As a result, people can prioritise the tasks that will allow them to live with certitude.

Becoming Your Own Best Friend

Throughout our lives there are circumstances where we need to uphold our values and decisions. Becoming your own best friend asserts your own self-reliance that will increase your ability to be informed of decisions that are best for you.

There are many circumstances throughout people's lives where they will need to face difficulties and solve them independently. In order to make conscientious decisions throughout your life, this can be achieved by being your own best friend, which will offer reliable frames of reference in evaluating circumstances.

Using your existing personal perspective along with an external viewpoint, you can then be informed of the most effective course of action.

To be your own best friend involves being conscious of your circumstances and emotions such that you are able to reinforce your ability to make optimal decisions. A person's thoughts affect their emotions as reflected from their negative bias, but their emotions also influence their thoughts.

Professor Noreena Hertz revealed that people who feel elated are increasingly willing to take more risks and are more generous and trusting. Correspondingly the experience of disappointment is associated with displeasure and fatigue that can lead to symptoms of depression.

Being your own best friend will allow you to carry out your own self-reflection so that you can become comprehensively informed of your emotions. You will then be able to address the present emotions by assimilating opposing statements that will moderate your frame of mind toward making proficient action.

For example, if you have been disappointed with your work performance and you are required to give a speech regarding the company's conducted research, it is likely that you will then experience uncertainty in your ability to deliver an effective speech performance.

By being your own confidant, you can be aware of your current sentiments such that by manifesting self-reinforcing thoughts, you can present the speech with confidence. Being able to regulate your thoughts and emotions allows you to improve your ability to live with an internal balance.

A person's outlook on life is significant toward shaping their capability to remain content. It is from the accumulation of one's frame of mind that shapes their perspective outlook. When a person is optimistic, this leads to anticipation of the future and develops the proclivity to live in the present moment.

Conversely, to remain indifferent in one's perspective outlook, people will experience negative circumstances that may lead to pessimism. From being your best friend, you are able to recognise when it is proficient to manifest a positive frame of mind which will allow you to maintain an optimistic outlook. This will lead to establishing your own contentment such that you are able to appreciate living in the present moment.

Through shaping an optimistic outlook while being able to regulate your thoughts and sentiments, you are then able to achieve an internal self-reliance. As a result, this refines your ability to make informed decisions that will allow you to live in a personal alignment.

From being your own best friend, you are able to increase your consciousness by including your external perspective to pursue the actions that have an optimal outcome. As a result of your own self-reliance, you are now able to live in contentment.

Gratitude

Gratitude originates from the Latin word *gratus*, referring to the qualities of "pleasing and thankful" toward devoted relationships, circumstances and life. In establishing gratitude, it is important not to focus on what you have already attained, but rather focus on what you can be grateful for.

From being informed about positive circumstances, the practice of gratitude will refine the expectations in your life. As a result, you will be able to reciprocate acts of kindness to others and that will allow you to remain content.

Steps to Practice Gratitude

1. Develop Mindfulness

Mindfulness involves opening your state of awareness to every aspect of the present experience, whether it is positive, negative or neutral. The positive experiences are opportunities to appreciate the circumstance while negative experiences are opportunities for future growth. Through such forming of silver linings, this reinforces your ability to focus on the present moment. From the practice of mindfulness, people are able to reduce any potential doubts and uncertainty, which will lead to the establishment of gratitude.

2. Exercise Meditation

Current society is filled with excess information that results in individuals becoming distracted, and it diverts their attention away from the present. Meditation involves the practice of filtering out unnecessary thoughts and sentiments so that individuals are free from their distractions. This allows people to live in the present at peace.

Through the practice of meditation, one is able to moderate their expectations toward focusing in the present and live with gratitude.

3. Express Your Gratefulness

Interacting with others goes beyond manners, courtesy and politeness. Individuals can express their gratefulness toward others by communicating and reciprocating their acts of kindness. This increases one's empathy and compassion which furthers their potential to living in the moment with a greater sense of self-appreciation.

4. Recall Grateful Experiences

Manifesting the experiences for which you are grateful will allow you to reinforce your gratitude. Through the practice of recalling grateful memories, you are able to recite your sentiments that will draw attention to all the experiences you are able to appreciate.

Gratitude is the quality that allows people to appreciate living in the present moment. It is from the appreciation of one's own experiences that shapes the expectations toward the areas of life they are grateful for.

Mindfulness and meditation strategies can also guide people to refine their clarity of thought. Correspondingly, the practice of gratefulness allows individuals to apply gratitude in their interactions with others such that they can recall the grateful experiences and appreciate them.

As a result of developing gratitude in your life, you are then capable of remaining content.

Key Points

1. The requirements to remain content include philosophical knowledge, which derives the reasons, ethics and values of human life.
2. The Greek philosopher Socrates outlines the reason of what is good and only that it can be derived from knowledge. Other people who act with ill intent have an intention that is perceived as good, but it is carried out in a contradictory manner.
3. Nelson Mandela was a South African political leader who led the movement to end racial segregation, and he united the nation toward the maintenance of peace.
4. From his active participation of the ANC, Mandela strived to oppose the apartheid laws by carrying out strikes, boycotts and protests.
5. After holding a rally in the City of Durban in 1952 that advocated nonviolent resistance toward racism, Mandela was arrested. During this same year, the ANC membership grew from 20,000 to 100,000.
6. While Mandela was in prison, sixty-nine unarmed citizens were killed, and 168 were injured during a protest opposing apartheid.
7. During the time Mandela was released in 1961, there were increasing tensions caused by the apartheid laws.
8. During a roadblock in Harwick, Mandela was arrested for leaving the country without a permit and inciting worker strikes in August 1962. An ANC hideout with arms and equipment were found during the same year and Mandela was tried on the count of sabotage.
9. In the defence proceedings, Mandela gave the "I Am Prepared to Die" speech that asserted the dedication of the South African people. The court found him guilty of sabotage and he was sentenced to life imprisonment.
10. During his sentence, the South African government offered Mandela several conditional releases which he repeatedly declined, citing the need of freedom of speech.
11. In February 1990, Nelson Mandela was released and after serving twenty-seven years in prison, he addressed the crowd on his focus to end apartheid. In 1993, Mandela received the Nobel Peace Prize for the termination of the apartheid regime.

12. Nelson Mandela was elected president of South Africa in 1994 and was responsible for implementing the national reconciliation council and socioeconomic reforms.
13. From following his conscience and being informed of the utilitarian perspective, the former South African president was able to foresee that every person deserves equal rights and opportunities.
14. Utilitarianism is a moral theory that outlines that the most ethical action is the one that results in the highest accumulation of utility or benefit for the greatest amount of people.
15. While there are specific forms of utilitarianism, what is of significance is for people, where possible, to choose the course of action that has the most utilitarian benefit toward others and society as a whole.
16. The Third-Person Analysis is a strategy that involves analysing the accumulated perspectives of the consequences of potential action. This allows people to make effective analysis which provides certainty in making decisions.
17. To be your own best friend increases your external perspectives such that you are able to undertake actions that are in alignment with your best interests.
18. Gratitude focuses on what a person is able to be grateful for rather than focusing on what they have already achieved.
19. The steps to establish gratitude include developing mindfulness, exercising meditation and applying and recalling the acts of gratefulness.
20. With your own self-reliance to make informed decisions, you are now aligned to attain the internal and external balance.

Chapter 9
Attaining the Twenty-First Century Balance

The journey to obtain balance in the twenty-first century is exemplified by the path undertaken by Henry Ford. His pursuit of making the automobile both reliable and affordable for the middle-class consumer encountered ongoing challenges.

Where his original financial backers and competitors focused on producing the automobile for the wealthy class, Henry Ford relied on his own to innovate. Before fulfilling his optimal goal, Ford improved the working conditions of his workers that furthered the progress of social equality in American society.

Henry Ford was born 30 July, 1863, on a farm in the state of Michigan during the phase of the second industrialisation. At the age of thirteen, Ford's father gave him a pocket watch and following his own curiosity, Henry often dismantled and reassembled the watch.

His neighbours and friends recognised his ability to fix timepieces and he earned a reputation as a watch repairman. Unsatisfied with work life at the farm that was manual and tedious, Ford left home and travelled to Detroit at the age of sixteen to become an apprentice in the machine workshops.

Ford came in contact with the internal combustion engine while being hired as a machinist working for James F Flower & Bros and Detroit Dry Dock Co. After three years away from the farm, Ford returned back to the family property where he began operating and servicing the Westinghouse portable steam engine.

The agriculture industry during this period was experiencing a transition from the previous reliance of horses to the integration of machinery-based farming methods.

Although Ford had a curiosity for the internal combustion engine and followed its progress, it was not until 1885 that he had his first opportunity to repair a gas-powered Otto engine. Two years later and after having acquired experience with the combustion engine, Ford designed his own version of the four-cycle Otto model.

Ford aimed to build this engine to determine whether he would understand the principles of the functioning parts that would later be used to replace the other manual machineries in his workshop.

While remaining on the farm, Ford's father offered him forty acres of timberland provided that he would give up being a machinist. With the marriage to his wife in 1888, Ford provisionally agreed to his father's terms and cut timber as his main occupation.

This provided the opportunity for Ford to read and work on the internal combustion engines while he was not working at his main occupation.

Henry Ford became a night engineer at the age of twenty-eight, working at the Edison Electric Illuminating Company. Although he was not initially experienced working in the electrical field, Ford saw his role as an opportunity to learn. Being promoted to chief engineer after two years, he had enough personal time to devote his attention to the experimentation of the internal combustion engine.

These experiments led to the completion of his first gasoline-powered four-wheeled vehicle which was named the Ford Quadricycle. He then sold this vehicle to get the sufficient financial support required to experiment on a lighter car. The second automobile built by Ford began to attract investors who had encouraged him to start a business.

Ford did not believe he was ready to start his own business until he had finished building his third vehicle that made improvements to its brakes and a water tank. Despite being offered a role as a general superintendent in the Edison Electric Illuminating Company, Ford left and established the Detroit Automobile Company.

One year after the company's inception in 1899 and with twelve investors, the first product produced was a delivery wagon. However, Ford was reluctant to place the vehicle in production until he perfected it to detail.

The parts required for the vehicle also proved problematic to source as the suppliers often delayed their shipments. Meanwhile, the stockholders were becoming restless and wanted immediate profitability.

Ford on the other hand wanted to create the perfect automobile. In 1901, these conflicts in values led the founders to dissolve the company.

A reorganised company referred to as the Henry Ford Company was established but they had further disputes with his financial backers. Ford left this organisation and devoted his attention to building the Ford 999 race car.

During this period, cars were considered luxuries and after Ford had been acquainted with Alexander Y Malcomson, discussions were made to build a motor vehicle that was accessible to the larger population.

A partnership was established and Henry began to design simple automobiles that were affordable. Along with other notable investors including Horace Elgin Dodge and John Francis Dodge, the partnership was reincorporated into the Ford Motor Company.

Launched in 1903, the company first built the Model A passenger vehicle that produced a daily assembling of single digit quantities. Being responsive from his previous business endeavours, Ford recognised that the production of cars had to be scaled in production in order to reduce the operational costs which would increase the production capacity.

This would drive down the cost of automobile production while the increase in sales would maintain the company's profitability. Ford first managed to reliably source many of the car parts from the Dodge brothers' workshops. This allowed Ford to focus on the development of new car designs that led to improvements made in the size, weight and utility.

As Ford finally became satisfied with the reliability of the Model T automobile, he then focused his attention on reducing the cost of the automobile. The vehicle assembly operation had proved to be a time constraint as the Ford Motor Company was now able to machine their parts efficiently.

Inspired by observing the de-assembling process of the moving meat carcasses in a meat packing facility, Ford recognised that implementing an assembly line would potentially improve the parts and vehicle assembly operations in his manufactory.

The Ford Motor Group in 1913 tested this assembly line experiment on the flywheel ignition component. Unlike the traditional method where the workers were required to assemble their own flywheel magneto.

Each worker was given the responsibility of installing several parts of the flywheel that would be placed onto the conveyor belt for the next task to be completed. The time to assemble each piece of flywheel dropped from twenty minutes to thirteen minutes.

As each part of the assembly line minimised the need for workers to move between other workshop locations, this had also reduced the logistical hazards within the factory.

With the success of the assembly line experiment on the flywheel, Ford engineers then incorporated the Model T motor and its transmission to be produced using the conveyor-belt system. By the end of 1913, all of the major components of the Model T were assembled using the assembly line process.

Ford then consistently improved the conveyor belt systems which led to the production of automobiles on a large scale. This allowed Ford to drop the price of the Model T by up to three times over the next two years from $850 to $360 (approximately $10,000 today).

Ford managed to make the automobile accessible to the average citizen which improved the mobility for people to travel throughout the nation. During the same period, the wages in 1914 for workers at the Ford Motor Company doubled from two dollars to five dollars a day while also reducing the daily working hours from nine hours to eight hours.

This had compelled other businesses to follow in response which improved the working conditions for the middle class. Through his own experience, Ford developed his capability to pursue his objectives that aligned with offering utilitarian benefits to society.

The Evaluation of Henry Ford

Henry Ford played an important role in the industrialisation of the twentieth century by improving the production processes in the automotive industry while also enhancing the working conditions for employees.

When his car competitors had perceived that automobiles were only accessible by the wealthy, Ford recognised an opportunity to scale the production of cars. This established his optimal goal and through his self-reliance and optimism, he upheld his creativity to innovate.

As a result, it was through Ford's perseverance of learning from his experiences that allowed him to produce automobiles that facilitated everyday transportation for the American people.

> Man is best educated who knows the greatest number of things that are so, and who can do the greatest number of things to help and heal the world.
> —Henry Ford

Henry Ford was an industrialist who took inspiration from his past mechanical experience in order to design and produce automobiles. The trajectory of Ford's life could have taken many notable turns if he did not remain persistent toward pursuing the utilitarian benefits of society.

Ford did have pressure to remain on the farm, however, he repeatedly turned back toward the experimentation and production of automobiles. Despite the failing of two business ventures, Ford perceived that, "Failure is simply the opportunity to begin again, this time more intelligently."

Through Ford's own optimism and self-reliance, this reinforced his ability to remain creative in his commitments, as was revealed through the scaling of his production process using the assembly line.

From such experimentation along with the Model T automobile already produced, Ford was then able to accomplish his utilitarian objectives.

In analysing the trajectory of Henry Ford, it is clear that he strived to provide well-rounded value by producing affordable and reliable automobiles. Ford's career path resembled his optimal goal of aligning his strengths with his cognitive interest such that he was able to create his own opportunities of designing and producing automobiles.

He initially experienced many challenges particularly within his business ventures and it was through reflecting from his own experiences that led him to establishing the right business relationships.

This allowed him to successfully establish the Ford Motor Company with partners who strived toward the same goals. It was then through Ford's own diligence to pursue his personal objectives that motivated him to persevere forward.

In summary, it was through Henry Ford's pursuit of his optimal goal that led to his self-reliance, which stimulated his creativity towards designing and producing automobiles.

Ford's career journey consisted of both setbacks and successes. It is from the outcome of Ford's endeavour that reduced the cost of automobiles, which made the passenger car a staple of the American culture. As a result Henry Ford was able to obtain his external balance.

Harmony

Harmony consists of achieving tranquillity between people's internal and external balance. To attain harmony involves living in the present while pursuing the objectives and living in the present state of peace.

The knowledge you have attained from the previous chapters 1 through 8 has guided you to refine your pursuits, expectations, beliefs and perceptions of the world. Now, you are able to utilise this knowledge to attain your internal and external balance.

To attain the external balance requires the need to establish the equilibrium between the expectations of your objective striving and the reality. From your own self-awareness, you are now informed of your skills and abilities that will allow you to establish optimal expectations toward achieving your goals.

While it is important to pursue your objectives, it is also pragmatic to pursue utilitarian commitments. The analysis of the historical figures such as the Wright brothers, Napoleon Bonaparte, Ludwig van Beethoven, Leonardo da Vinci, Nelson Mandela and Henry Ford provides references for the shaping of expectations in the undertaking of your pursuits.

These experiences allow you to refine your expectations such that you are focused towards channelling your energies to fulfil your objectives.

From the initial desire to accomplish the objectives, it is anticipated that people will set high levels of expectations. However, the uncertainty and experimentation stages of any pursuit are inevitable.

Hence, during the pursuit of your objectives, it is optimal to refine your expectations during the phase of change such that it reinforces your motivation to accomplish goals.

Utilising strategies to regulate your thoughts and sentiments facilitates the shaping of expectations in accordance with the reality. As you are in alignment with channelling your energies to complete your objectives, you have now attained the external balance.

When you are not completing your commitments, shift your perceptions to the internal state of mind. The acts of gratitude and compassion will direct you to accept and appreciate who you are so that you can live at peace.

With your ability to regulate your expectations, thoughts and perspective outlook, you can address your uncertainties. By practicing mindfulness and meditation, you are then able to be cognisant of when your mind experiences any deviations from living in the present moment.

As a result of utilising these strategies, this refines the conscious awareness, which allows you to live in an internal balance.

To achieve a consistent state of the internal balance does not require the pursuit of any externalities. Instead, this involves being self-aware of when you are experiencing distractions and addressing them to maintain the state of peace.

Through being in the homogenous state of the internal balance, people are able to refine their consciousness to make optimal decisions. With this increase in mindfulness, the raising of your own consciousness will direct you to maintain your internal balance.

Now that you have attained your internal and external balance, you will become increasingly aware of when you will experience any deviations from this state of harmony.

Figure 14–Harmony and External and Internal Balance

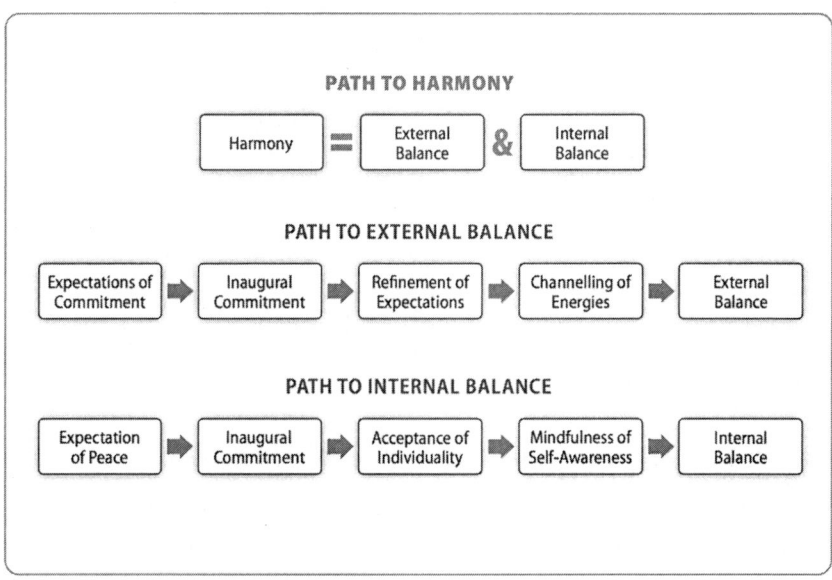

While the path to achieve this tranquil state may be perceived as not challenging from the figure above, each path has required diligence in assimilating the knowledge to become yours.

As circumstances change throughout your life, it is from your capability of re-applying the strategies outlined from this book that will allow you to consistently attain harmony.

Conclusion

Progress Forward from Here

Your journey of attaining the twenty-first century balance has now been complete. Now that you are living in the external and internal balance, the principles and strategies you have applied will guide you toward the goals you have aspired to achieve.

Since the world has changed faster in the last twenty years than the last century, it is necessary for people to also progress forward. In an increasingly technology-centred world where the ability to obtain relevant knowledge has never been this readily available, you are now able to make informed actions that will lead to the achievement of your objectives.

It is natural for humans to strive toward furthering their desires. This is psychologically explained from hedonic adaptation, which outlines the human tendency to return to the equilibrium state after experiencing an emotional response from the experience of circumstances.

Many people seek to attain balance throughout their lives but do not know where to begin. It is from such periods where one decides to question their uncertainty which initiates their use of self-reliance to finding the solution.

Through reading this book, people are able to recognise which objectives are worthwhile to strive toward, and that will align towards living in harmony. From this journey to attain balance, I hope you have enjoyed the narrations of the Industrial Revolution and the Dark Ages, along with the stories of historical figures.

Research in the fields of psychology, neurology and philosophy has been included within the content in order to complement the analysis and strategies presented in this book.

Now that you have attained your own balance, I wish you the best of luck in living a meaningful and fulfilled life.

If you would like to learn more or contact me, visit my website https://marklaw.net. There is a community of like-minded people who would also like to discuss any future challenges ahead.

References

Introduction: The Purpose for Balance

Armine, Michael. "Atomic Education Urged by Einstein." *New York Times*, May 25, 1946. Interview with Albert Einstein quote.

World Bank. "Decline of Global Extreme Poverty Continues but Has Slowed: World Bank." World Bank, 2018. https://www.worldbank.org/en/news/press-release/2018/09/19/decline-of-global-extreme-poverty-continues-but-has-slowed-world-bank.

Chapter 1: What Makes You Most Happy

Brickman, Philip, Dan Coates and Ronnie Janoff-Bulman. "Lottery Winners and Accident Victims: Is Happiness Relative?" *Journal of Personality and Social Psychology* 36, no. 8 (1978): 917–27.
https://doi.org/10.1037//0022-3514.36.8.917. Researchers from North-western University.

Clark, Andrew E, Paul Frijters and Michael A Shields. "Relative Income, Happiness and Utility: An Explanation for the Easterlin Paradox and Other Puzzles." *Relative Income, Happiness and Utility: An Explanation for the Easterlin Paradox and Other Puzzles (June 2007). IZA Discussion Paper No. 2840*, June 2007, 1–36.
https://papers.ssrn.com/sol3/papers.cfm?abstract_id=998225. Institute of Labour Economics in Germany.

"Definition of Happiness." Merriam-webster.com. Merriam-Webster, updated March 24 2020. https://www.merriam-webster.com/dictionary/happiness.

"'Depression: Let's Talk' Says WHO, as Depression Tops List of Causes of Ill Health." www.who.int. World Health Organisation, March 30, 2017. https://www.who.int/news-room/detail/30-03-2017--depression-let-s-talk-says-who-as-depression-tops-list-of-causes-of-ill-health. Estimate figures from the World Health Organisation.

"Dr Isha Gupta (Duggal), Neurologist in New York | US News Doctors." Usnews.com, 2013. https://health.usnews.com/doctors/isha-gupta-46564. Specialty / Subspecialties.

Dunn, Elizabeth W, Lara B Aknin and Michael I Norton. "Spending Money on Others Promotes Happiness." *Science* 319, no. 5870 (March 21, 2008): 1687–88. https://doi.org/10.1126/science.1150952.

Fredrickson, Barbara L and Daniel Kahneman. "Duration Neglect in Retrospective Evaluations of Affective Episodes." *Journal of Personality and Social Psychology* 65, no. 1 (1993): 45–55. https://doi.org/10.1037/0022-3514.65.1.45. Research leading to proposal of peak-end rule.

Helliwell, J, R Layard and J Sachs. "World Happiness Report 2018." New York: Sustainable Development Solutions Network, 2018.

Helliwell, J, R Layard, J Sachs, J De Neve, L Aknin and S Wang. "World Happiness Report 2022." New York: Sustainable Development Solutions Network, 2022.

Kahneman, Daniel, Barbara L Fredrickson, Charles A Schreiber and Donald A Redelmeier. "When More Pain Is Preferred to Less: Adding a Better End." *Psychological Science* 4, no. 6 (November 1993): 401–5. https://doi.org/10.1111/j.1467-9280.1993.tb00589.x. Research leading to peak-end rule.

Kahneman, Daniel and Amos Tversky. *Choices, Values and Frames*. 1st ed. New York: Cambridge University Press, 2000. Peak End Rule.

MacLeod, Andrew K and Clare Conway. "Well-being and the Anticipation of Future Positive Experiences: The Role of Income, Social Networks and Planning Ability." *Cognition & Emotion* 19, no. 3 (March 2005): 357–74. https://doi.org/10.1080/02699930441000247.

Ortiz-Ospina, Esteban and Max Roser. "Happiness and Life Satisfaction." Our World in Data, updated May 2017. https://ourworldindata.org/happiness-and-life-satisfaction. Gallup world poll graph of self-reported life satisfaction versus gross domestic product per capita, Latin America finding.

Romeo, Melodie. *From Glory to Glory*. Balboa Press, 2019. Compassion quote from psychologist Paul Gilbert.

Rosenbloom, Stephanie. "But Will It Make You Happy?" *The New York Times*, August 7, 2010. https://www.nytimes.com/2010/08/08/business/08consume.html?pagewanted=all. Hedonic adaptation.

Shin, Dol C and Dan Johnson. "Avowed Happiness as an Overall Assessment of the Quality of Life." *Social Indicators Research* 5, no. 1–4 (1978): 475–92. https://doi.org/10.1007/bf00352944. Table 2, stepwise multiple regression of happiness.

Spector, Nicole. "Smiling Can Trick Your Brain into Happiness—and Boost Your Health." NBC News. NBC News, updated January 10, 2018. https://www.nbcnews.com/better/health/smiling-can-trick-your-brain-happiness-boost-your-health-ncna822591.

Spoon, Marianne. "Training Compassion 'Muscle' May Boost Brain's Resilience to Others' Suffering." University of Wisconsin-Madison, May 18, 2018. https://news.wisc.edu/training-compassion-muscle-may-boost-brains-resilience-to-others-suffering/.

Waldinger, Robert. "What Makes a Good Life? Lessons from the Longest Study on Happiness." Ted.com. TED Talks, November 2015.

https://www.ted.com/talks/robert_waldinger_what_makes_a_good_life_lessons_from_the_longest_study_on_happiness?language=en. 5:39.

Wallis, Claudia. "The New Science of Happiness." *Time Magazine* January 9, 2005. http://www.paultrapnell.com/stories/TheNewScienceOfHappiness.html. Time poll, Feeling Good in the United States.

Weiss, Alexander, James E King, Miho Inoue-Murayama, Tetsuro Matsuzawa and Andrew J Oswald. "Evidence for a Midlife Crisis in Great Apes Consistent with the U-Shape in Human Well-Being." *Proceedings of the National Academy of Sciences* 109, no. 49 (November 19, 2012): 19949–52. https://doi.org/10.1073/pnas.1212592109.

Weng, Helen Y, Andrew S Fox, Alexander J Shackman, Diane E Stodola, Jessica Z K Caldwell, Matthew C Olson, Gregory M Rogers and Richard J Davidson. "Compassion Training Alters Altruism and Neural Responses to Suffering." *Psychological Science* 24, no. 7 (May 21, 2013): 1171–80. https://doi.org/10.1177/0956797612469537.

Chapter 2: Social Media Renaissance

Chambers, Deborah. *Social Media and Personal Relationships Online Intimacies and Networked Friendship*. Palgrave Macmillan, 2013.

Cherry, Kandra. "How Social Comparison Theory Influences Our Views on Ourselves." VeryWellMind. Dotdash, updated September 23, 2019. https://www.verywellmind.com/what-is-the-social-comparison-process-2795872.

Descartes, René. *The Philosophical Writings of Descartes: Volume 1*. Translated by John Cottingham, Robert Stoothoff and Dugald Murdoch. New York: Cambridge University Press, 1984.

Descartes, René. *The Philosophical Writings of Descartes: Volume 2*. Translated by John Cottingham, Robert Stoothoff and Dugald Murdoch. New York: Cambridge University Press, 1985.

Dwyer, Kate. "The Renaissance Roots of Social Media." Hyperallergic, April 4, 2018. https://hyperallergic.com/436009/the-renaissance-roots-of-social-media/.

Eyal, Nir. *Hooked: How to Build Habit-Forming Products*. Penguin, 2014. Product habit and addictions.

Eysenck, Hans J and Michael H Eysenck. *Personality and Individual Differences: A Natural Science Approach*. New York: Plenum, 1985.

Festinger, Leon. "A Theory of Social Comparison Processes." *Human Relations* 7, no. 2 (1954): 117–40. https://doi.org/10.1177/001872675400700202. First impressions based off upward or lower social comparison.

Hay, William W and Greg Wray. *Experimenting on a Small Planet: A History of Scientific Discoveries, a Future of Climate Change and Global Warming*. Switzerland: Springer, 2016. Cartesian coordinate system.

Haynes, Trevor. "Dopamine, Smartphones & You: A Battle for Your Time." Science in the News, May 1, 2018. http://sitn.hms.harvard.edu/flash/2018/dopamine-smartphones-battle-time/.

Hunt, Melissa G, Rachel Marx, Courtney Lipson and Jordyn Young. "No More FOMO: Limiting Social Media Decreases Loneliness and Depression." *Journal of Social and Clinical Psychology* 37, no. 10 (December 2018): 751–68. https://doi.org/10.1521/jscp.2018.37.10.751.

JR Thorpe. "Can An Introvert Become an Extrovert? We Asked Psychologists How It's Done." Bustle, 20 March 2020. https://www.bustle.com/p/can-introvert-become-extrovert-we-asked-psychologists-how-its-done-18161747. Joshua Kaplow source.

Lieberman, Matthew D *Social: Why Our Brains Are Wired to Connect*. Crown, 2013.

Massimo Rospocher and Bronwen Wilson. *Beyond the Public Sphere: Opinions, Publics, Spaces in Early Modern Europe*. Duncker & Humblot GmbH, 2012. alba amicorum history and uses.

Migala, Jessica. "What It Means to Be an Ambivert, and How to Know If You Are One." Health.com, December 18, 2018. https://www.health.com/mind-body/ambivert-definition. Barry Smith ambiversion.

Newman, Lex. "Descartes' Epistemology (Stanford Encyclopaedia of Philosophy)." In *Stanford.Edu*, February 15, 2019. https://plato.stanford.edu/entries/descartes-epistemology/.

O'halloran, Kay L, Bradley A Smith and Volker J Eisenlauer. *Multimodal Studies : Exploring Issues and Domains*. New York: Routledge, 2011. Part 2 section 8 on social media.

Penenberg, Adam L "Digital Oxytocin: How Trust Keeps Facebook, Twitter Humming." Fast Company, July 18, 2011. https://www.fastcompany.com/1767125/digital-oxytocin-how-trust-keeps-facebook-twitter-humming. Paul Zak's third experiment.

Poel, Dieuwke, Louis Peter Grijp and Wim Van Anrooij. *Identity, Intertextuality and Performance in Early Modern Song Culture*. Brill, 2016. Uses of Alba Amicorum.

Ricci, Jeanne. "The Growing Case for Social Media Addiction CSU." Calstate.edu. The California State University, June 28, 2018. https://www2.calstate.edu/csu-system/news/Pages/Social-Media-Addiction.aspx.

Seabrook, Elizabeth M, Margaret L Kern and Nikki S Rickard. "Social Networking Sites, Depression and Anxiety: A Systematic Review." *JMIR Mental Health* 3, no. 4 (November 23, 2016): e50. https://doi.org/10.2196/mental.5842.

Williams, Bernard. *Descartes the Project of Pure Enquiry*. Routledge, 2005.

Williston, Byron and André Gombay. *Passion and Virtue in Descartes*. New York: Humanity Books, 2003.

Chapter 3: The Optimal Goal Strategy

Ammianus Marcellinus. *The Later Roman Empire (AD 354-78)*. Translated by Walter Hamilton. New York, NY: Penguin Classics, 2004.

Asbridge, Thomas S *The First Crusade: A New History*. New York: Oxford University Press, 2005. P7-24.

Asplund, Jim and Nikki Blacksmith. "The Secret of Higher Performance." Gallup.com. Gallup, May 3, 2011. https://news.gallup.com/businessjournal/147383/secret-higher-performance.aspx. Gallup poll on productivity performance.

Bradberry, Travis and Jean Greaves. *Emotional Intelligence 2.0*. San Diego, Calif.: Talentsmart, 2009.

Diamond, Jared. *Collapse: How Societies Choose to Fail or Succeed.* New York: Penguin Books, 2011. Collapse of Roman Empire.

Dwyer, Philip. *Napoleon: The Path to Power, 1769-1799*. London: Bloomsbury, 2007. P132-135 Siege of Toulon.

Godechot, Jacques. "Napoleon I | Biography, Achievements, & Facts." In *Encyclopædia Britannica*, January 10, 2019. https://www.britannica.com/biography/Napoleon-I.

Goleman, Daniel. *Emotional Intelligence: Why It Can Matter More than IQ*. London: Bloomsbury, 2010.

Harvard Business Review. *Self-Awareness (HBR Emotional Intelligence Series)*. Boston, Massachusetts: Harvard Business Review Press, 2018.

History.com Editors. "Napoleon Bonaparte." History. A&E Television Networks, updated April 8, 2020. https://www.history.com/topics/france/napoleon. rank to brigadier general.

History.com Editors. "Nikola Tesla." History. A&E Television Networks, updated March 13, 2020. https://www.history.com/topics/inventions/nikola-tesla.

King, Gilbert. "The Rise and Fall of Nikola Tesla and His Tower." Smithsonian. Smithsonian.com, February 4, 2013. https://www.smithsonianmag.com/history/the-rise-and-fall-of-nikola-tesla-and-his-tower-11074324/.

Mclynn, Frank. *Napoleon : A Biography*. New York: Arcade Pub, 2011. Early Life.

Monfort, Mary, Samuel A Martin and William Frederickson. "Information-Processing Differences and Laterality of Students from Different Colleges and Disciplines." *Perceptual and Motor Skills* 70, no. 1 (February 1, 1990): 163–72. https://doi.org/10.2466/pms.1990.70.1.163. Research on left-right brain.

Nikola Tesla. *The Inventions, Researches and Writings of Nikola Tesla*. Edited by Thomas Commerford Martin. San Diego: Canterbury Classics, 2019.

OECD. *Understanding the Brain: Toward a New Learning Science*. Cambridge: OECD Publishing, 2002. Chapter 4 Section 6.

Roberts, Andrew. *Napoleon: A Life*. Penguin Books, 2015.

Rose, Chris. *Self-Awareness and Personal Development: Resources for Psychotherapists and Counsellors*. Basingstoke, New York: Palgrave Macmillan, 2012.

Seligman, Martin. *Authentic Happiness: Using the New Positive Psychology to Realise Your Potential for Lasting Fulfilment*. New York: Free Press. (2002). Quote p249.

Tesla, Nikola. *My Inventions and Other Writings*. Dover Publications, 2016. P27 Alternating current vision.

Wasson, Donald L "Fall of the Western Roman Empire." In *Ancient History Encyclopaedia*. Ancient History Encyclopaedia, April 12, 2018. https://www.ancient.eu/article/835/fall-of-the-western-roman-empire/.

Chapter 4: The Balance of Change

Adler, Alfred. *Understanding Human Nature. transl. ed.* Martino Fine Books, 2010. People change in their social relationships for self-improvement.

Allen, Robert C *The British Industrial Revolution in Global Perspective*. Cambridge: Cambridge University Press, 2009. Agricultural improvements.

Ashton, T S *The Industrial Revolution, 1760-1830*. 2nd ed. Oxford University Press, 1998.

Covey, Stephen R *7 Habits of Highly Effective People*. Anniversary Edition. Simon & Schuster, 2013.

Drucker, Peter F *Managing in a Time of Great Change*. Boston, Ma: Harvard Business Review Press, 2009.

Dweck, Carol S "What Having a 'Growth Mindset' Actually Means.", January 13, 2016.
https://hbr.org/2016/01/what-having-a-growth-mindset-actually-means.

Dweck, Carol S *Mindset: The New Psychology of Success*. New York: Random House, 2007.

Fox, Stephen. "Situated Learning Theory versus Traditional Cognitive Learning Theory: Why Management Education Should Not Ignore Management Learning." *Systems Practice* 10, no. 6 (December 1997): 727–47.
https://doi.org/10.1007/bf02557922.

Heifetz, Ronald A, Alexander Grashow and Martin Linsky. *The Practice of Adaptive Leadership: Tools and Tactics for Changing Your Organisation and the World*. Harvard Business Press, 2009.

Hiatt, Jeffrey M and Timothy J Creasey. *Change Management : The People Side of Change*. Loveland, Colorado: Prosci Learning Centre Publications, 2012.

Hoffman, Edward. *The Right to Be Human: A Biography of Abraham Maslow*. Subsequent edition. McGraw-Hill, 1999.

Horn, Jeff, Leonard N Rosenband and Merritt Roe Smith, eds. *Reconceptualising the Industrial Revolution*. The MIT Press, 2010.

Ichirō Kishimi and Fumitake Koga. *The Courage to Be Disliked: The Japanese Phenomenon That Shows You How to Change Your Life and Achieve Real Happiness*. Atria Books, 2018.

International Monetary Fund. *World Economic Outlook, April 2018: Cyclical Upswing, Structural Change*. Washington, DC: International Monetary Fund, 2018. P177 for patents and G5.

International Monetary Fund. "World Economic Outlook, April 2018 Cyclical Upswing, Structural Change." *Https://Www.Imf.Org/En/Publications/WEO/Issues/2018/03/20/~/Media/Files/ Publications/WEO/2018/April/Text.Ashx?La=en*. Washington, DC: International Monetary Fund, April 2018.

Kotter, John P *Leading Change*. Harvard Business School Press, 2013.

Lally, Phillippa, Cornelia H M van Jaarsveld, Henry W Potts and Jane Wardle. "How Are Habits Formed: Modelling Habit Formation in the Real World." *European Journal of Social Psychology* 40, no. 6 (October 2010): 998–1009. https://doi.org/10.1002/ejsp.674.

Lave, Jean. "Teaching, as Learning, in Practice." *Mind, Culture and Activity* 3, no. 3 (July 1996): 149–64. https://doi.org/10.1207/s15327884mca0303_2.

Lave, Jean and Etienne Wenger. *Situated Learning : Legitimate Peripheral Participation*. First. Cambridge University Press, 1991.

"Learning Theories." Uoregon.edu. Accessed March 8, 2019. http://otec.uoregon.edu/learning_theory.htm#SituatedLearning. Constructivism in traditional learning.

Miller, George A "The Magical Number Seven, plus or Minus Two: Some Limits on Our Capacity for Processing Information." *Psychological Review* 101, no. 2 (1994): 343–52. https://doi.org/10.1037/0033-295X.101.2.343.

Mohajan, Haradhan Kumar. "The First Industrial Revolution: Creation of a New Global Human Era." *Journal of Social Sciences and Humanities* 5, no. 4 (2019): 377–87.
https://mpra.ub.uni-muenchen.de/96644/1/MPRA_paper_96644.pdf

Nederveen Pieterse, Jan. "Twenty-First Century Globalisation: A New Development Era." *Forum for Development Studies* 39, no. 3 (August 2, 2012): 367–85. https://doi.org/10.1080/08039410.2012.688859.

Nentwig, Peter and David Waddington. *Making It Relevant: Context Based Learning of Science*. Münster: Waxmann, 2005. P15-17 Situated Learning.

Saccenti, Edoardo, Age K Smilde and Will H M Saris. "Beethoven's Deafness and His Three Styles." *BMJ* 343, no. d7589 (November 2011): d7589–d7589. https://doi.org/10.1136/bmj.d7589. Researchers from Amsterdam's Swammerdam Institute for Life Sciences.

Shuttleworth, Jennifer. "SAE Standards News: J3016 Automated-Driving Graphic." Sae Mobilus. Sae Mobilus, updated January 7, 2019.
https://www.sae.org/news/2019/01/sae-updates-j3016-automated-driving-graphic. Six levels of driving autonomy.

Swafford, Jan. *Beethoven: Anguish and Triumph*. First edition. Houghton Mifflin Harcourt, 2015.

The Editors of Encyclopaedia Britannica. "Industrial Revolution | Definition, Facts, & Summary." In *Encyclopædia Britannica*, October 9, 2018. https://www.britannica.com/event/Industrial-Revolution.

Chapter 5: Inspire Yourself or Who Will?

Bandura, Albert. "Self-Efficacy: Toward a Unifying Theory of Behavioural Change." *Advances in Behaviour Research and Therapy* 1, no. 4 (1978): 131–61. https://doi.org/10.1037//0033-295x.84.2.191.

Branden, Nathaniel. *The Psychology of Self-Esteem: A Revolutionary Approach to Self-Understanding That Launched a New Era in Modern Psychology*. New York: Jossey-Bass Inc, 2001.

Crouch, Tom D *First Flight: The Wright Brothers and the Invention of the Airplane*. Government Printing Office, 2002. P18 upbringing environment quote.

Cuddy, Amy. "Transcript of 'Your Body Language May Shape Who You Are'." Ted.com. TED Talks, 2012. https://www.ted.com/talks/amy_cuddy_your_body_language_may_shape_who_you_are/transcript. Body language from 7:58.

Ericsson, K Anders, Ralf Th Krampe and Clemens Tesch-Romer. "The Role of Deliberate Practice in the Acquisition of Expert Performance." *Psychological Review* 100, no. 3 (1993): 363–406. https://doi.org/10.1037/0033-295x.100.3.363. Factors affecting confidence.

Freedman, Russell. *The Wright Brothers: How They Invented the Airplane*. Reissue edition. New York: House Holiday Inc, 2007.

Goldsmith, Kelly and Ravi Dhar. "Incentive Framing and Task Motivation: The Intuitive Appeal of Gains and the Actual Efficacy of Losses." *SSRN Electronic Journal*, 2011. https://doi.org/10.2139/ssrn.1817902.

Harter, Susan. "Effectance Motivation Reconsidered Toward a Developmental Model." *Human Development* 21, no. 1 (1978): 34–64. https://doi.org/10.1159/000271574.

History.com Editors. "Wright Brothers." History, updated June 19, 2019. https://www.history.com/topics/inventions/wright-brothers.

Ito, Tiffany A, Jeff T Larsen, N Kyle Smith and John T Cacioppo. "Negative Information Weighs More Heavily on the Brain: The Negativity Bias in Evaluative Categorisations." *Journal of Personality and Social Psychology* 75, no. 4 (1998): 887–900. https://doi.org/10.1037/0022-3514.75.4.887. Negative bias source.

Kuhl, Julius. "A Theory of Self-Regulation: Action versus State Orientation, Self-Discrimination and Some Applications." *Applied Psychology* 41, no. 2 (January 2008): 97–129. https://doi.org/10.1111/j.1464-0597.1992.tb00688.x. Self-regulation.

McCullough, David. *The Wright Brothers. Wright-Brothers.Org*. Reprint Simon & Schuster, 2016.

Nicholls, John G "Achievement Motivation: Conceptions of Ability, Subjective Experience, Task Choice and Performance." *Psychological Review* 91, no. 3 (1984): 328–46. https://doi.org/10.1037//0033-295x.91.3.328.

Peper, Erik, Annette Booiman, I-Mei Lin and Richard Harvey. "Increase Strength and Mood with Posture." *Biofeedback* 44, no. 2 (June 2016): 66–72. https://doi.org/10.5298/1081-5937-44.2.04. Body language.

Reid, Jill M *Creating Peace of Mind: Focusing on What Matters in a Changing World*. Authorhouse, 2016. Not accepting the presumably truths quote.

Sadhana Damani and Larissa Clay. *Resolving Relationship Difficulties with CBT: A Self-Help Guide for Couples*. Blue Stallion Publications, 2008. Positive reinforcement.

Wright, Orville and Wilbur Wright. *The Early History of the Airplane*, 2008. Orville quoting flying as a sport.

Chapter 6: The Enhanced Perspective

Aristotle. *The Nicomachean Ethics*. Edited by Lesley Brown. Translated by David Ross. New edition. Oxford University Press, 2009.

Briggs, Asa. *The Age of Improvement, 1783-1867*. 2nd ed. Routledge, 1999. Victorian morality.

Capra, Fritjof. *Learning from Leonardo: Decoding the Notebooks of a Genius*. Berrett-Koehler Publishers, 2013.

Capra, Fritjof. *The Science of Leonardo: Inside the Mind of the Great Genius of the Renaissance*. Knopf Doubleday Publishing Group, 2007. P3 quote on painting, P161 quote on scientific method.

Cherry, Kendra. "How the Availability Heuristic Affects Your Decision Making." VeryWellMind, 2019. https://www.verywellmind.com/availability-heuristic-2794824.

Cloud, Henry and John Townsend. *Boundaries: When to Say Yes, How to Say No to Take Control of Your Life*. Grand Rapids, Michigan: Zondervan, 2017. Valued qualities in relationships.

Finucane, Melissa L, Ali Alhakami, Paul Slovic and Stephen M Johnson. "The Affect Heuristic in Judgments of Risks and Benefits." *Journal of Behavioural Decision Making* 13, no. 1 (January 2000): 1–17. https://doi.org/10.1002/(SICI)1099-0771(200001/03)13:1<1::AID-BDM333>3.0.CO;2-S.

Flanagan, Owen J and Amélie Oksenberg Rorty. *Identity, Character and Morality: Essays in Moral Psychology*. Cambridge, Mass.: MIT Press, 1990.

Garrett, Elisabeth. "The Socratic Method | University of Chicago Law School." Uchicago.edu. The Green Bag Inc (check), 2019. https://www.law.uchicago.edu/socratic-method.

Himmelfarb, Gertrude. *The De-Moralisation of Society: From Victorian Virtues to Modern Values*. New York: Alfred A Knopf, 1995. Character values between societies.

Isaacson, Walter. *Leonardo da Vinci: The Biography*. Simon & Schuster, 2017. Overview.

Jahn, Gary R "The Aesthetic Theory of Leo Tolstoy's What Is Art?" *The Journal of Aesthetics and Art Criticism* 34, no. 1 (1975): 59–65. https://doi.org/10.2307/428645.

Jarrat, Susan C *Rereading the Sophists: Classical Rhetoric Refigured*. Carbondale, Ill.; Edwardsville, Ill.: Southern Illinois University Press, 2001. Socratic method.

Marshall Vian Summers. *Relationships and Higher Purpose: Finding Your People, Place and Purpose in the World*. New Knowledge Library, 2014.

Michalewicz, Zbigniew and David B Fogel. *How to Solve It: Modern Heuristics*. 2nd ed. Springer Berlin Heidelberg, 2004.

Paul, Richard and Linda Elder. *The Thinker's Guide to the Art of Socratic Questioning*. Tomales, Calif.: Foundation for Critical Thinking, 2016.

Tolstoy, Leo. *Anna Karenina*. Translated by Constance Garnett. Simon and Schuster, 2010. Quotes on P5, 206, 1169 and 1170.

Tolstoy, Leo. *Death Of Ivan Ilyich*. UK edition. London: Penguin Books, 2017.

Tolstoy, Leo. *War and Peace*. Translated by Louise Maude and Aylmer Maude. Hertfordshire: Wordsworth Editions, 1993.

Tolstoy, Leo. *What Is Art?* rev. ed. London: Penguin Books, 1996.

Tversky, Amos and D Daniel Kahneman. "Judgment under Uncertainty: Heuristics and Biases." *Science* 185, no. 4157 (September 27, 1974): 1124–31. https://doi.org/10.1126/science.185.4157.1124. Background research.

Tversky, Amos and Daniel Kahneman. "Availability: A Heuristic for Judging Frequency and Probability." *Cognitive Psychology* 5, no. 2 (September 1973): 207–32. https://doi.org/10.1016/0010-0285(73)90033-9.

Chapter 7: Emphasise Your Belief System

Aurelius, Marcus. *Meditations*. Translated by George Long. Courier Corporation, 1997. Book 8, No.47 quote on what we can control.

Aurelius, Marcus, Plato and Aristotle. *The Modern Library Collection of Greek and Roman Philosophy 3-Book Bundle: Meditations; Selected Dialogues of Plato; The Basic Works of Aristotle*. Random House Publishing Group, 2012. Book 4 of Mediations No. 49a quotation of obstacles by Marcus Aurelius.

Goldsmith, Kelly and Ravi Dhar. "Incentive Framing and Task Motivation: The Intuitive Appeal of Gains and the Actual Efficacy of Losses." *SSRN Electronic Journal*, 2011. https://doi.org/10.2139/ssrn.1817902. (repeat)

Diogenes Laertius. *The Lives and Opinions of Eminent Philosophers*. Translated by Charles Duke Yonge. Andesite Press, 2015. Zeno of Citium overview knowledge.

Graver, Margaret. *Stoicism & Emotion*. University of Chicago Press, 2008.

Heckhausen, Jutta. "Evolutionary Perspectives on Human Motivation." *American Behavioural Scientist* 43, no. 6 (March 2000): 1015–29. https://doi.org/10.1177/00027640021955739.

Hodge, Joanna. *Heidegger and Ethics*. Routledge, 1995. Nihilism and belief systems.

Holiday, Ryan and Stephen Hanselman. *Daily Stoic: 366 Meditations on Self-Mastery, Perseverance and Wisdom: Featuring New Translations of Seneca, Marcus Aurelius and Epictetus*. Profile Books, 2016. August 26th Zeno shipwreck quote, January 5th quote from Seneca.

Maslow, Abraham H "A Theory of Human Motivation." *Psychological Review* 50, no. 4 (1943): 370–96. https://doi.org/doi.org/10.1037/h0054346.

Murguia, Edward and Kim Diaz. "The Philosophical Foundations of Cognitive Behavioural Therapy: Stoicism, Buddhism, Taoism and Existentialism." *Journal of Evidence-Based Psychotherapies* 15, no. 1 (2015): 37–50.

Naish, John. *Enough*. Hachette UK, 2012. Marcus Aurelius appreciative on life quote.

Nietzsche, Friedrich. *Will To Power*. Edited by Walter Kaufmann. Translated by Walter Kaufmann and RJ Hollingdale. New York: Random House, 1968. Quotation on beliefs made on Spring-Fall 1887.

Pascal Boyer. *Minds Make Societies: How Cognition Explains the World Humans Create*. Yale University Press, 2018.

Pigliucci, Massimo. "Stoicism | Internet Encyclopaedia of Philosophy." In *Utm.Edu*. Accessed October 16, 2018. https://www.iep.utm.edu/stoicism/.

Robertson (chapter in book check), Donald. *The Routledge Handbook of the Stoic Tradition*. Edited by John Sellars. London: Routledge, Taylor & Francis Group, 2017. Cognitive behavioural therapy influenced by stoicism.

Robertson, Donald. *How to Think Like a Roman Emperor: The Stoic Philosophy of Marcus Aurelius*. New York: St Martin's Press, 2019.

Salzgeber, Jonas. *The Little Book of Stoicism: Timeless Wisdom to Gain Resilience, Confidence and Calmness*, 2019. P30 Epictetus quote on practicing stoicism.

Saunders, Shaun, Don Munro and Miles Bore. "Maslow's Hierarchy of Needs and Its Relationship with Psychological Health and Materialism." *South Pacific Journal of Psychology* 10, no. 2 (1998): 15–25. https://doi.org/10.1017/s0257543400000833.

William Braxton Irvine. *A Guide to the Good Life: The Ancient Art of Stoic Joy*. Oxford University Press, 2009. Stoic beliefs.

Wooldridge, Frosty. *Living Your Spectacular Life*. Authorhouse, 2017. Quote from Epictetus on character development.

Chapter 8: How You Can Remain Content

Allen, Summer. "The Science of Gratitude," May 2018. Whitepaper (check prepared for the John Templeton Foundation by the Greater Good Science Centre at UC Berkeley).

Barnard, Rita. *The Cambridge Companion to Nelson Mandela*. Cambridge University Press, 2014.

Brickhouse, Thomas C and Nicholas D Smith. *Plato's Socrates*. Reprint. Oxford University Press, 1996.

Driver, Julia. "The History of Utilitarianism." Stanford.edu, updated September 14 2014. https://plato.stanford.edu/entries/utilitarianism-history/.

Duignan, Brian and Henry R West. "Utilitarianism Philosophy." In *Encyclopædia Britannica*, updated May 12, 2015. https://www.britannica.com/topic/utilitarianism-philosophy.

Emerson Waldo, Ralph. *Self-Reliance and Other Essays*. New York: Dover Publications Inc., 1994.

Emmons, Robert A and Cheryl A Crumpler. "Gratitude as a Human Strength: Appraising the Evidence." *Journal of Social and Clinical Psychology* 19, no. 1 (March 2000): 56–69. https://doi.org/10.1521/jscp.2000.19.1.56.

Hain, Peter. *Mandela: The Concise Story of Nelson Mandela*. Spruce, 2010.

Hertz, Noreena. "Asleep at the Wheel: What Makes Us Human Is Our Irrationality." Newstatesman.com, 2014. https://www.newstatesman.com/2014/08/asleep-wheel-what-makes-us-human-our-irrationality?page=13. Quote on elation and risk.

Laertius, Diogenes. *Lives of the Eminent Philosophers*. Translated by RD Hicks. Harvard University Press, 1979. Quote Socrates quote on knowledge book 2 chapter 5 [31].

Mandela, Nelson. *Conversations with Myself.* Reprint Picador, 2011. check (foreword by Barrack Obama), letter with former wife.

Mandela, Nelson. "I Am Prepared to Die." Opening of defence proceeding court case in the IP Trial presented at the Rivonia Trail, n.d. http://db.nelsonmandela.org/speeches/pub_view.asp?pg=item&ItemID=NMS0 10. Quote from Rivonia Trail.

Mandela, Nelson. *Long Walk to Freedom: The Autobiography of Nelson Mandela.* Boston: Back Bay Books, 1995. Overall overview on Nelson Mandela.

Mandela, Nelson. *Nelson Mandela and the End of Apartheid*. Edited by Sahm Venter. WW Norton & Co, 2018. Foreword by Zamaswazi Dlamini-Mandela.

Mandela, Nelson. Nelson Mandela interview with John Battersby of the Christian Science Monitor. Interview by John Battersby, 2000. http://www.mandela.gov.za/mandela_speeches/2000/000210_battersby.htm. Nelson Mandela quote on change.

Marušić, Iris, Denis Bratko and Predrag Zarevski. "Self-Reliance and Some Personality Traits: Sex Differences." *Personality and Individual Differences* 19, no. 6 (December 1995): 941–43. https://doi.org/10.1016/s0191-8869(95)00118-2.

Mill, John Stuart. *Utilitarianism*. Edited by George Sher. Cambridge, MA: Hackett Publishing Co, Inc, 2002.

"South African History Online." South African History Online, 2019. https://www.sahistory.org.za/. Timeline information.
Vlastos, Gregory. *Socrates: Ironist and Moral Philosopher*. Cornell University Press, 1991. Analysis of moral and ethics of Socrates.

Wood, Alex M, Stephen Joseph and John Maltby. "Gratitude Predicts Psychological Well-Being above the Big Five Facets." *Personality and Individual Differences* 46, no. 4 (March 2009): 443–47. https://doi.org/10.1016/j.paid.2008.11.012.

Chapter 9: Attaining the Twenty-First Century Balance

Aristotle. *The Nicomachean Ethics*. Edited by Lesley Brown. Translated by David Ross. New edition. Oxford University Press, 2009. (repeat)

Ford, Henry. *Today and Tomorrow: Commemorative Edition of Ford's 1926 Classic. Rev. Ed.* Taylor & Francis Inc, 1988.

Ford, Henry and Fay Leone Faurote. *My Philosophy of Industry*. 1929. Reprint, Literary Licensing, 2013.

Ford, Henry and SBP Editors. *My Life and Work*. Samaira Book Publishers, 2017.

Gailliot, Matthew T "Happiness as Surplus or Freely Available Energy." *Psychology* 03, no. 09 (September 25, 2012): 702–12. https://doi.org/10.4236/psych.2012.39107.

Gelderman, Carol W "Henry Ford | Biography, Education, Inventions, & Facts." In *Encyclopædia Britannica,* July 26, 2018. https://www.britannica.com/biography/Henry-Ford.

"Henry Ford Quotes-The Henry Ford." Thehenryford.org, October 27, 2015. https://www.thehenryford.org/collections-and-research/digital-resources/popular-topics/henry-ford-quotes/. Quote on Ford toward education.

History.com Editors. "Ford Factory Workers Get 40-Hour Week." History, July 28, 2019. https://www.history.com/this-day-in-history/ford-factory-workers-get-40-hour-week. 1914 salary improvement.

John, Anthony. *The Aristotelian Ethics: A Study of the Relationship between the Eudemian and Nicomachean Ethics of Aristotle*. Oxford University Press, 1978.

Lykken, David and Auke Tellegen. "Happiness Is a Stochastic Phenomenon." *Psychological Science* 7, no. 3 (1996): 186–89. https://doi.org/10.1111/j.1467-9280.1996.tb00355.x. Psychological research on happiness levels over time.

Polansky, Ronald. *Cambridge Companion to Aristotle's Nicomachean Ethics*. New York: Cambridge University Press, 2014.

Reeves, CDC *Practices of Reason: Aristotle's Nicomachean Ethics*. New York: Oxford University Press, 1992.

Conclusion

Brickman, Philip, Dan Coates and Ronnie Janoff-Bulman. "Lottery Winners and Accident Victims: Is Happiness Relative?" *Journal of Personality and Social Psychology* 36, no. 8 (1978): 917–27. https://doi.org/10.1037//0022-3514.36.8.917. Researchers from North-Western University. (repeat)

Lykken, David and Auke Tellegen. "Happiness Is a Stochastic Phenomenon." *Psychological Science* 7, no. 3 (1996): 186–89. https://doi.org/10.1111/j.1467-9280.1996.tb00355.x. Psychological research on happiness levels over time. (repeat)

Rosenbloom, Stephanie. "But Will It Make You Happy?" *The New York Times*, August 7, 2010. (repeat) https://www.nytimes.com/2010/08/08/business/08consume.html?pagewanted=all. Hedonic adaptation.